COMBAT AIRCRAFT

151 HARRIER GR 7/9 UNITS
IN COMBAT

SERIES EDITOR TONY HOLMES

151

COMBAT AIRCRAFT

Michael Napier

HARRIER GR 7/9 UNITS IN COMBAT

OSPREY
PUBLISHING

OSPREY PUBLISHING

Bloomsbury Publishing Plc

Kemp House, Chawley Park, Cumnor Hill, Oxford OX2 9PH, UK

29 Earlsfort Terrace, Dublin 2, Ireland

1385 Broadway, 5th Floor, New York, NY 10018, USA

E-mail; info@ospreypublishing.com

www.ospreypublishing.com

OSPREY is a trademark of Osprey Publishing Ltd

First published in Great Britain in 2023

A catalogue record for this book is available from the British Library.

ISBN; PB 9781472857613; eBook 9781472857606; ePDF 9781472857637; XML 9781472857620

23 24 25 26 27 10 9 8 7 6 5 4 3 2 1

Edited by Tony Holmes
Cover Artwork by Gareth Hector
Aircraft Profiles by Janusz Światłoń
Index by Alison Worthington
Typeset by PDQ Digital Media Solutions, UK
Printed and bound in India by Replika Press Private Ltd

Osprey Publishing supports the Woodland Trust, the UK's leading woodland conservation charity.

To find out more about our authors and books visit **www.ospreypublishing.com**. Here you will find extracts, author interviews, details of forthcoming events and the option to sign up for our newsletter.

Acknowledgements

I am very grateful to the following indivduals for their contributions to this book – Stuart Atha, Martin 'Benny' Ball, Lee Barton (RAF Air Historical Branch), Simon Blake (Jaguar), Mike Hile, Mark 'Dins' Linney, Dunc Mason, Alex Muskett (Jaguar), Steve Phillips, Al Pinner, Ashley Stevenson, Andrew Suddards, Ian 'Cab' Townsend, Simon Turner, Pat 'PV' Voigt and Mark Zanker.

Front Cover

On 30 August 1995 Flt Lt Mark 'Dins' Linney of No 4 Sqn, flying Harrier GR 7 ZG434, released two 1000-lb Paveway II Laser-Guided Bombs against the Serbian ammunition storage depot at Hadzici, west of Sarajevo. These were the first weapons to be dropped operationally by the RAF Harrier GR 7 force. Linney's wingman on this mission was Flt Lt Pat 'PV' Voigt in Harrier GR 7 ZG500, and the target was laser-designated by Flt Lt Simon Blake of No 6 Sqn in Jaguar XX962 using a GEC-Ferranti Thermal Imaging Airborne Laser Designation Pod (*Cover Artwork by Gareth Hector*)

Previous Pages

A Harrier GR 7 circles over Albania while waiting to be cleared into the airspace over Kosovo by the strike controller aboard the Airborne Battlefield Command and Control Center aircraft during a CAS mission for Operation *Engadine* in 1999. It is loaded with four RBL755 cluster bombs and two AIM-9L Sidewinders, the latter mounted on BOL rails. Often, the weather conditions over Kosovo would prevent Harriers from entering the airspace (*Mark Zanker*)

CONTENTS

INTRODUCTION

Developed from the Hawker P 1127 and Kestrel experimental aircraft of the early 1960s, the Hawker Siddeley Harrier GR 1 entered Royal Air Force (RAF) service with No 1 Sqn at Wittering, in what was then Huntingdonshire, in July 1969. Three more Harrier squadrons followed at Wildenrath, in Germany – No 4 Sqn in April 1970, No 20 Sqn in December 1970 and No 3 Sqn in January 1972.

The heart of the Harrier was the Rolls-Royce Pegasus Mk 101/102 engine, which, thanks to its vectored thrust, gave the aircraft a Vertical Take Off and Landing capability, although, because of the limits on hover performance, in practice the Harrier used a Short Take Off and Vertical Landing (VSTOL) profile. Thus freed from the constraints of using vulnerable airfields, the Harrier could operate from remote semi-prepared airstrips, giving it unrivalled flexibility. Dispersed operating sites were also difficult to detect and more secure against counter-attack than traditional airfields.

During the early 1970s, the Harrier GR 3 variant was introduced, featuring a more powerful Pegasus Mk 103 engine, a Ferranti Laser Ranger and Marked Target Seeker and a Radar Warning Receiver (RWR). Some 40 of these aircraft were manufactured as GR 3s, and another 62 GR 1 airframes were modified to GR 3 standard. A high accident rate in the early days of Harrier operations bore witness to the fact that the type was a demanding aeroplane to fly, so the RAF adopted the policy of selecting only its best pilots

Harrier GR 9 ZG477 of No 4 Sqn over Afghanistan in November 2008. The ultimate development of the Harrier, the GR 9 variant was a potent, flexible and extremely effective weapons platform. By the time the aircraft was prematurely withdrawn from service, the type had been flying almost continuously on operational deployments over Iraq, the Balkans and Afghanistan for the previous 16 years. This particular aircraft now resides in the RAF Museum at Hendon, in London (*Crown Copyright/MoD*) to fly the Harrier. As a result, the squadrons equipped with the aircraft soon gained a reputation as an elite force within the RAF, and Harrier pilots were regarded by other aircrew with a mixture of admiration and envy.

The Harrier squadrons in Germany were fully declared to the Allied Air Forces Central Europe, 2nd Allied Tactical Air Force and tasked with the Close Air Support (CAS) of the NATO Northern Army Group. Their main target would be Soviet armour and their chief weapon was the Hunting BL755 cluster bomb. The RAF Germany squadrons moved from Wildenrath to Gutersloh in 1977 to bring them closer to their expected wartime deployment areas.

Meanwhile, No 1 Sqn was earmarked to support the Allied Command Europe Mobile Force, which was expected to deploy to Norway in time of war. The unit was also available to meet British national tasks – in 1975, Harriers deployed to Belize, in Central America, to guard against an invasion of the country by Guatemala, and the Harrier force subsequently retained a permanent presence there until 1993. In 1982, Harriers from No 1 Sqn flew from the aircraft carrier HMS *Hermes* during the Falklands conflict, supporting British troops as they advanced from San Carlos towards Port Stanley.

The Harrier GR 3 proved to be very effective in its role, and Harrier pilot Sqn Ldr S Phillips later remarked that 'it was a great aircraft for CAS at a high sortie rate using field sites – six trips before lunch was commonplace, and the Army units I worked with really valued our support'.

However, for all the ingenuity of its design, the uniqueness of its performance, the skill of its operators and the originality of its employment, the Harrier was, in practice, limited to short-range daylight operations. The aircraft's modest weight-carrying capacity governed both its weapons load and tactical range, and by the early 1980s it was clear to the RAF that greater range and weapon loads were needed. It was clear, too, that the Harrier might be needed to expand its role into air interdiction and possibly even move from low-level into the medium-level airspace. This need for a more versatile machine was shared by the US Marine Corps, which was also a major Harrier operator with a fleet of some 110 AV-8As. In fact, it was the US Marine Corps that initiated the development of a more capable variant of the Harrier, which became the McDonnell Douglas/British Aerospace AV-8B Harrier II.

Compared to the original Harrier, the Harrier II benefitted from 20 years' worth of advances in engine, structural and avionic technologies. The aircraft was powered by the Pratt & Whitney F402-RR-406 rated at 22,000 lbs of thrust, which delivered nearly five per cent more power than the Mk 103 fitted in the earlier Harriers. Around a quarter of the aircraft's structure was made of composite materials, generating a weight saving which in turn allowed for the incorporation of more complex avionics and extra weapons stations.

The RAF was initially reluctant to join the Harrier II programme, since it had a modest requirement of just 60 aircraft, in comparison to the US Marine Corps' need for more than 300 aircraft. However, the Harrier GR 5 – a version of the AV-8B modified to suit RAF needs (and fitted with the Rolls-Royce Pegasus Mk 105/106) – was procured, and it entered service with No 1 Sqn in October 1988.

Apart from improved performance, the new Harrier II incorporated an Angle Rate Bombing System (ARBS), which was well suited to medium-level operations, the Marconi Zeus Electronic Countermeasures (ECM) system and a Plessey Missile Approach Warning (MAW) system. Despite these differences, Maj M Hile, who flew both the AV-8B with the US Marine Corps and the GR 7 on an exchange posting with No 4 Sqn, reckoned that 'from an aircraft perspective, handling and avionics differences between the US Marine Corps AV-8B+ and the GR 7 were minimal. From planning systems to avionics [including Hands-On Throttle And Stick (HOTAS)], to performance, the aircraft and compatibilities were similar'.

Although the Harrier GR 5 represented a major enhancement in operational capability when compared to earlier variants, it had been overtaken by events and was obsolescent even as it entered service. Rapid advances in Electro-Optics (EO) enabled ground forces to continue combat through the hours of darkness, generating a requirement for CAS by night as well as by day. A true combat-ready replacement for the Harrier GR 3 would need Forward Looking Infra-Red sensors and a cockpit that was fully compatible with Night Vision Goggles (NVGs). This configuration – although initially not with a combat capability – came with the introduction of the Harrier GR 7 to Nos 3 and 4 Sqns in 1990.

Eventually, some 41 Harrier GR 5s and 21 Harrier GR 5As (GR 5 variants with the wiring for the GR 7 systems) were converted to GR 7 standard, and a further ten aircraft were built from scratch as GR 7s. Of this total, 30 airframes were further modified in 2003 by the incorporation of the Pegasus Mk 107 engine, delivering ten per cent more power, to become the GR 7A.

After receiving the Harrier GR 7, the squadrons undertook the intensive work-up that was necessary to master single-seat night EO operations. This coincided with the programme to gain approval for various equipment configurations and weapons loads – something that had already been started with the GR 5. It was during this period, in 1992, that Germany-based Nos 3 and 4 Sqns moved from Gutersloh to Laarbruch. The Harrier force achieved a night combat-ready status in 1993, and the operational deployments that soon followed marked the start of almost continuous combat operations for the next 15 years. At this point, the Air Order of Battle of frontline RAF Harrier GR 7 units was as follows:

RAF Strike Command	
No 1 Group	
Wittering	No 1 Sqn
No 2 Group	
Laarbruch	No 3 Sqn
	No 4 Sqn

In addition to practising operating from austere airstrips, the Harrier GR 7 force regularly flew from the Royal Navy aircraft carriers HMS *Invincible*, HMS *Illustrious* and HMS *Ark Royal*.

With the closure of Laarbruch in 1999 and Wittering in 2000, the Harrier force was relocated to Cottesmore, in Rutland. At this stage the Joint Force Harrier was established at Cottesmore, placing both RAF

Armed with CRV7 rocket pods and 500-lb Paveway IV LGBs, Harrier GR 9A ZG511 drops back from a tanker after taking on fuel during a mission over Afghanistan in December 2008. It is also carrying an AN/AAQ-33 Sniper Advanced Targeting Pod and DJRP on its under-fuselage pylons (*Crown Copyright/MoD*)

Harrier GR 7 and Royal Navy Sea Harrier FA 2 units under the single command of No 3 Group RAF.

Continuous updates in response to operational requirements saw the integration of the GEC Marconi Thermal Imaging and Laser Designation (TIALD) targeting pod, as well as the procurement of the Bristol Aerospace CRV7 rocket and Raytheon AGM-65G2 Maverick guided missile. A further significant upgrade to capabilities came between 2006 and 2009 with the conversion of 68 GR 7/7A aircraft to GR 9/9A standard. This included the fitting of a Military Standard 1760 databus, a new main computer, updated weapon management software and further improved avionics. The obsolescent TIALD pod was replaced by the Lockheed Martin Sniper AN/AAQ-3 Advanced Targeting Pod, and the Harrier GR 9 was also made capable of using the AGM-114 Hellfire air-to-ground missile, Advanced Short Range Air-to-Air Missile and Paveway IV Laser/GPS (Global Positioning System) Guided Bomb.

A further change in the line-up occurred in 2006, when the Sea Harrier FA 2 was withdrawn from service. At the same time, No 3 Sqn converted to the Typhoon and its Harriers were passed on to 800 Naval Air Squadron (NAS). In a streamlining of the command structure, the Joint Force Harrier (JFH) was transferred to No 2 Group and the Air Order of Battle of frontline Harrier GR 7/9 units was as follows:

RAF Air Command	
No 2 Group	
Cottesmore	No 1 Sqn
	No 4 Sqn
	800 NAS (retitled Naval Strike Wing in 2007)

This Order of Battle was maintained until 31 March 2010 when No 4 Sqn disbanded. This was followed shortly thereafter by the unexpectedly early withdrawal of the Harrier II from RAF service, a decision driven by a budgetary crisis at the Ministry of Defence (MoD) rather than operational considerations. After becoming combat-ready in the mid-1990s, the Harrier GR 7/9 force was involved in almost continuous combat operations over the Balkans, Iraq and Afghanistan, serving with great distinction until the aircraft was withdrawn from service in January 2011.

CHAPTER ONE

NORTHERN IRAQ AND BELIZE

OPERATION *WARDEN*

In the aftermath of the first Gulf War, a rebellion by Kurdish separatists in northern Iraq was put down by Iraqi forces, leading to a humanitarian crisis in the region. In response to the UN Security Council Resolution 688 condemning 'the repression of the Iraqi civilian population in Kurdish-populated areas', a Coalition comprising the USA, Britain and France, with Turkish support, established a No-Fly Zone (NFZ) over northern Iraq in April 1991. The NFZ was intended to prevent Iraqi forces from operating aircraft north of the 36th Parallel against the Kurdish population.

The Coalition operation to enforce the NFZ had the overall codename Operation *Provide Comfort*, and the British component, which was responsible for tactical reconnaissance of the area, was known as Operation *Warden*. Initially, the aircraft for Operation *Warden* came from Nos 6, 41 and 54 Sqns, which provided detachments to operate four Jaguar GR 1s from the Turkish Air Force base at Incirlik, on the outskirts of Adana in southwest Turkey.

The Jaguar force was relieved by six Harrier GR 7s in April 1993. It is perhaps ironic that after completing a three-year work-up for the demanding night low-level attack role, the first operational deployment for the Harrier GR 7 force should be for a medium-level daytime reconnaissance role. Nevertheless, over the next two years, each Harrier squadron took its turn to man the detachment at Incirlik for a three-month period. Within

Harrier GR7 ZG474 undertakes an Operation *Warden* sortie over northern Iraq, the aircraft carrying a Phimat chaff dispensing pod on the left outboard pylon and two CBU-87 cluster bombs and two 2000-lb external fuel tanks on the other underwing pylons. It is also armed with AIM-9L Sidewinders for self-protection. Most Operation *Warden* sorties were carried out at medium-level so as to remain clear from the threat of small arms fire. Typical sortie lengths were between 2 hr 45 min and 3 hr 30 min, although on occasions longer sorties were flown. Aircraft always flew in at least pairs in order to give each other cross-cover (*Mark Linney*)

A formation of Harrier GR 7s accompanied by a VC10K tanker from No 101 Sqn transit from their base at Incirlik, near Adana in southern Turkey, towards the Operation *Warden* operating area over northern Iraq. Each pair of aircraft would take turns refuelling during the 45-minute flight towards the Iraqi border, ensuring that they entered the operational area with a full fuel load (*Andrew Suddards*)

that time individual pilots would deploy for six weeks, although the groundcrew spent the entire three months in Turkey. Aircraft for the operation were pooled from all the Harrier units, so that each squadron retained enough aeroplanes to keep the 'rear party' flying at their home base during their tenure of Operation *Warden*. The number of Harriers deployed to Incirlik was increased to eight aircraft in 1994.

Because they were operating predominantly at medium-level while on operations, rather than at low-level as they were in Britain or Germany, the Harriers were resprayed in a light grey Alkali Removable Temporary Finish (ARTF) paint scheme which offered better camouflage at higher altitudes. Aircraft at Incirlik were also marked with a two-letter tail code, the first letter of which was a 'W' indicating 'Warden'.

The first unit to deploy to Incirlik was No 4 Sqn, which arrived in-theatre in early April. The first operational mission over Iraq was flown by Wg Cdr D A Harwood and Flt Lt A C Pinner, who were accompanied by a Jaguar, on 5 April 1993.

On a typical Operation *Warden* mission, four aircraft would launch, supported by a VC10K air-to-air refuelling (AAR) tanker for a mission which would last around 2 hrs 45 min (although sorties of three-and-a-half hours would later become routine). After a 400-mile transit eastwards along the Turkish–Syrian border, the formation would reach the Iraqi border over the Zagros mountains about 70 miles north of Mosul. From here the Harriers entered the NFZ to carry out their reconnaissance tasking. While they were operating in the NFZ, Coalition aircraft were restricted to flying above 5000 ft to keep them clear of small arms fire, although low flying was permitted in defined 'safe areas' which were under Kurdish control.

'One of our tasks was to show presence to the Kurds', commented Flt Lt M V Linney, a pilot with No 4 Sqn, 'and we did this by flying up and down Mosul or Erbil high streets at full power and zero feet. We also had to use the old GR 3 recce pod – this was a low-level optimised system that was useless at altitude. Even after the hard deck went up to 5000 ft we still used to nip down to get the imagery tasked'.

'The flying over Northern Iraq was repetitive and routine', commented Sqn Ldr I MacDonald, a Flight Commander with No 1 Sqn. 'A long transit through Turkey followed by a medium/high level recce run to continually monitor targets of interest. We flew as part of a large Combined Force Mission with tanker support under the umbrella of the Americans. The medium- and high-level airspace was well sanitised, and we obviously knew the locations of SAM [Surface-to-Air Missile] sites. Our missions were flown at medium- and high-level around the SAM sites and above small arms and MANPADS [Man-portable air defence systems]'.

According to Flt Lt S C Turner, a pilot with No 1 Sqn, 'operational theatres like the Northern NFZ presented very real threats to military aircraft. There were various SAMs, MANPADs, AAA [anti-aircraft artillery] and numerous small arms threats from a widespread distribution of Russian weaponry. The Iraqi regime encouraged their troops with a financial reward for shooting down a Coalition aircraft, which led to a variety of engagements, including an SA-3 launch. Indeed, one of our Harrier GR 7s had its canopy smashed

As it banks away, a Harrier GR 7 shows a typical weapon load for a mission over northern Iraq. It carries a Phimat chaff dispensing pod on the left outboard pylon and two CBU-87 cluster bombs and two 2000-lb external fuel tanks on the other underwing pylons. Again, the aircraft is armed with AIM-9Ls for self-protection. It also carries an old Harrier GR 3 Vinten reconnaissance pod on the centreline station (*Andrew Suddards*)

when hit with a glancing blow by a Kalashnikov round (assumed). Other exchanges resulted in HARM [High-speed Anti-Radiation Missile] being fired at SA-3 sites following missile launches – the winner in this exchange was the HARM, and the SA-3 site was destroyed. I guess no rewards were paid to that soldier!'

A complication to the overall situation in northern Iraq was the ambiguous nature of Turkish participation in the operation, for Turkey was simultaneously fighting its own campaign against a Kurdish terrorist insurgency. Indeed, the very towns and villages that Operation *Warden* sought to protect from Iraqi forces also provided bases to Kurdish separatists who were carrying out guerrilla attacks in Turkey. Thus it was not uncommon for Turkey to cancel Coalition operations into Iraq while they carried out their own missions, although on occasions Harrier pilots saw Turkish Air Force aircraft delivering weapons on to Kurdish settlements. 'I actually witnessed some Turkish F-4s that were doing high-angle dive-bombing on targets in Kurdistan', reported Flt Lt Linney.

By now the Coalition efforts had been renamed Operation *Northern Watch* (distinguishing them from Operation *Southern Watch*, which covered the southernmost part of Iraq from bases in Saudi Arabia). The British component retained the national designation Operation *Warden*, however.

The daily missions mounted into the northern NFZ were flown in 'packages' typically comprising 30 to 40 aircraft, including reconnaissance and offensive support aircraft, fighter escorts and AAR tanker support. As well as the VC10K, Harrier pilots sometimes found themselves refuelling from other AAR tankers from various NATO countries, including USAF KC-135s equipped with the Boom-Drogue Assembly and C-135FRs of the *Armée de l'Air*. Operation *Northern Watch* packages were invariably escorted by dual-role USAF F-15Es, which were always first in and last out of the operational area.

The standard load for the Harrier for an Operation *Warden* sortie included two 2000-lb (300 gallon) underwing fuel tanks, two AIM-9L Sidewinder air-to-air missiles, two CBU-87 Combined Effects Munitions (CEM) cluster bombs, a Phimat chaff dispenser pod and a reconnaissance pod.

A pair of fully armed F-15E Strike Eagles from the 48th Operations Group's 492nd Fighter Squadron formate on Harrier GR 7 ZG505 on the return leg from an Operation *Warden* sortie over northern Iraq. The Harrier is fitted with a Vinten reconnaissance pod that was originally procured for the Harrier GR 3. The F-15Es, which shared Incirlik with the Harrier force in-theatre, provided fighter cover while the RAF aircraft were in Iraqi airspace (*Andrew Suddards*)

As Flt Lt S D Atha, a pilot with No 4 Sqn, explained, the reconnaissance pod was an 'old GR 3 recce pod [that was] dusted off and rushed back into service on the GR 7. The GR 3 pods were optimised for low-level flying and had five cameras of varying focal lengths that provided "horizon-to-horizon" coverage. At the heights being flown it was only the outer cameras pointing just below the wingtips that could provide photographs of useable resolution. Yet again innovation was required.

'With a 20-degree field-of-view and the need to reduce slant range, pilots had to conduct a knife edge manoeuvre past targets (guided by lines drawn using chinagraph pencils on the aircraft canopy) to have any hope of producing photographs of sufficient quality to allow the highly talented imagery analysts eagerly waiting back at Incirlik to exploit the photographs for scraps of intelligence about the Iraqi Army. Frustrations were further compounded by ever present oil smears on the camera lenses (oil leaks, sadly, were an enduring challenge for the Harrier, regardless of mark). Somehow, despite an abundance of challenges, outstanding photographs were produced using the GR 3 pod, including images of Iraqi barracks and the Roland SAM sites around the city of Mosul and its nearby dam.'

Nor was the reconnaissance pod the only item of equipment that was not entirely suited to medium-level operations – the integral Zeus ECM system was also optimised for low-level flying, and, therefore, did not look below the aircraft. 'This meant', continued Flt Lt Atha, 'there was a "black hole of ignorance" beneath the Harrier that became bigger the higher you flew. In this void, the enemy radars could find and target the Harrier GR 7 without any warning from Zeus. The only way to fill the gap was to regularly weave as a pair of aircraft, constantly checking each other's "six-o'clock" below as well as behind'. The situation was further complicated by not infrequent spurious warnings from Zeus which were triggered by other aircraft or the Iraqi telephone network.

The use of the CBU-87 was also driven by the fact that the British-built BL755 was intended for low-level delivery. While the CBU-87 could be physically dropped by the Harrier GR 7, the weapon aiming system did not have the ballistic figures needed to generate an accurate bombsight. So, according to Atha, 'the Qualified Weapon Instructors (QWIs) pulled out their calculators and trigonometric tables and quickly came up with a series of tables and delivery profiles that acted as a bridge between UK and US weapon performance'.

Although Operation *Warden* missions were usually planned with AAR support, thanks to 'Harrier pilot ingenuity' any lack of a tanker did not necessarily mean that the aircraft could not fulfil their mission. Flt Lt Linney recalled an occasion when 'our tanker

Harrier GR 7 ZD380 leads a flight of four aircraft, each of which are carrying four external fuel tanks and a single reconnaissance pod. During Operation *Warden*, this configuration gave the Harrier sufficient range to carry out reconnaissance tasks without AAR if no tanker support was available on the day (*Mark Linney*)

went unserviceable and the French – we used to tank off the French sometimes – didn't have any availability, so the Boss and I worked out that we could actually go from Incirlik into the area, do our photography and come back out again in a four-tank fit with Sidewinders, because obviously we wanted some self-defence capability. We took off the CBUs that we would normally carry and put on an extra tank. We had the aircraft doing this mega- mission of three or four hours in the four-tank fit with Sidewinders and a reconnaissance pod. The test pilots at Boscombe Down got wind of this and said that that configuration was not in the Release to Service. They had a real whinge to us about it and we replied along the lines of "well we've done it and it works!"'

On 23 November 1993, three pairs of Harriers from No 4 Sqn launched for a reconnaissance mission in the NFZ. The transit, in company with the VC10K tanker, was carried out above a thick layer of cloud stretching from 10,000 ft up to 25,000 ft. Some 45 minutes into the transit, the leading pair, comprising Sqn Ldrs S Forward and J Fernie, were about to complete their refuelling in preparation for pushing into the NFZ with full tanks. Waiting for his turn to refuel, Flt Lt Linney was flying close off the wing of Sqn Ldr Fernie when 'suddenly I saw a mass of flame shooting out of his intake and the aircraft was surrounded by fire, then it dropped straight into the clouds'. Fernie had experienced a spectacular engine surge, and soon after shutting down the engine in an attempt to clear the surge, he entered the cloud. Acutely aware that he was heading towards mountainous terrain, he attempted to relight the engine but could not restart it.

Meanwhile, Forward, concerned for the safety of his wingman, also descended through the cloud. 'Thanks to a mixture of courage and skill', recalled Flt Lt Atha, 'Forward emerged into an Iraqi valley and hauled his GR 7 through gaps between the ground and the clouds, desperate for any sign of Fernie. Above the cloud, the remaining four Harrier pilots maintained a silent presence alongside the tanker aircraft, uttering not a word, listening to the emergency radio frequency on which they hoped that Fernie would call, using the emergency radio attached to his combat vest'.

Fernie broke cloud just as he reached the minimum safety altitude at 10,000 ft, but after another futile attempt to relight the engine, he was forced to eject just 1500 ft above the high ground, coming down near Sirsenk, about 50 miles north of Mosul. Here, he was taken under the protection of Kurdish Peshmerga fighters until he was rescued shortly afterwards by US Special Forces (SF) and the USAF 305th Rescue Squadron. Over the next weeks, the wreckage of the aircraft was recovered piece by piece, including the ejection seat, which was already being used as a seat in a nearby village hut.

On 14 April 1994, Harrier pilots were witnesses to another unfortunate incident. 'On the day in question', recalled Sqn Ldr MacDonald, 'I had just exited northern Iraq to begin the long transit home. I was flying in a pair. There had been a fair bit of operational chatter, so we were aware there was something going on. Just after exiting Iraq, AWACS informed us two "Hinds" [Mil Mi-24 gunship helicopters] had been shot down, and they tasked us to carry out a recce of the crash site. This was obviously an exciting development, so we took on more fuel from the tanker and re-briefed.

'Our simple plan was to fly over the coordinates at high-level taking pictures, followed by a rapid descent in a "safe area" to ultra-low level for a second recce run. We had often discussed tactics during the tour, and decided there was no middle ground when it came to heights. It was either well above small arms/MANPADS or "on the deck". We duly flew over the target area at height, "all cameras blazing". Our return run was flown at ultra-low-level over the target in a battle pair, remaining low until we reached the border with Turkey. We did not see any wreckage, although I recollect the other pilot did see some smoke. The low-level recce was operationally sound (and, in the event, produced pictures confirming the aircraft as UH-60 Black Hawks).

'The mission was very exhilarating, and we were "on a high" when we were met back at Incirlik by the RAF Commander (group captain rank) and a very serious looking US Army major. We were not invited to view our films with the group captain and the major, but it was obvious something was up.'

In fact, the F-15s had shot down two US Army UH-60 Black Hawks in error.

Although Iraqi troops, complete with anti-aircraft weapons, were active above the 36th Parallel, Coalition aircraft were not routinely challenged in the NFZ. But that is not to say that the airspace over northern Iraq – even when flying above supposedly friendly areas – was not without danger. On 2 February 1995, four Harriers from No 1 Sqn were tasked with locating artillery pieces that were thought to be hidden in a large swathe of Kurdish-controlled territory around Erbil. As they entered Iraq, the formation split into two pairs to carry out the search, with Flt Lt Atha leading N J W Ingle in the first pair and Wg Cdr D Walker (Officer Commanding (OC) No 1 Sqn) leading Flt Lt P W Wharmby in the second. Because they were flying over an ostensibly friendly area, the search had been planned at low-level.

During the first sweep through the area, the lead pair found a Soviet-built D-20 152 mm gun-howitzer. As they performed a second sweep, the Wg Cdr Walker's canopy shattered, spraying the pilot with shards of Perspex. Accompanied by his wingman, Walker climbed away from the ground, and with the help of their supporting VC10K tanker, the two aircraft were able to divert to a nearby airfield in Turkey. Once safely down, Wg Cdr Walker commandeered Wharmby's Harrier and returned to Incirlik. It seems likely that he had overflown a Kurdish wedding or similar event where it was customary for the attendees to celebrate by their firing guns into the air.

A Harrier GR 7 flies past the partly-destroyed observatory in the mountains to the northeast of Erbil during an Operation *Warden* sortie in October 1994. Although the Harrier was technically at 'low-level' when this photograph was taken, it was actually flying at 7000 ft above sea level (*Mark Linney*)

Flt Lt Turner recalled another memorable sortie the following month;

'Further into this detachment, I was leading our daily eight-ship of Harrier GR 7s (integrated into the usual "package" of around 35 aircraft). We were tasked to recce a variety of targets, including Mosul airfield. The plan had been to use our medium altitude recce pod, equipped with a left oblique-looking camera with a zoom lens. This allowed photos to be taken from around 15,000 ft, above the main threats, but required a precise lateral offset – normally around a few miles from the target but entirely dependent on the height above target.

'Our plan, which had to be carefully drawn out and accurately executed, had been to run eastbound on a track to the south of the target with four pairs in battle formation, trailing each other with around 30 seconds of spacing. However, on ingress, we could clearly see a very large thunderstorm in the area to the south of the target that would prevent us from flying the plan (we would have been in cloud had we stuck to the pre-briefed plan). Rather than abort this part of the mission, I elected to deliver an airborne re-brief of the run.

'Our aircraft were also equipped with a low-level recce pod with five cameras giving coverage of everything under the aircraft from horizon to horizon. However, we were not normally supposed to fly at low-level, or even below 5000 ft. So now that we were planning to fly low, our original formation increased our vulnerability to the small arms threat. So again, we re-briefed to make our last 90-degree turn on to our eastbound track a simultaneous event. This resulted in a formation in line abreast, or wall of eight in our case, with around one mile between each aircraft, closing to about half-a-mile over the airfield.

'For the recce run, we accelerated to our highest speed at full power, and descended to around 100 ft above the ground. With the airfield providing us with such a large target, we ran all eight recce pods when overhead it.

Harrier GR 7 ZG503 undertakes an Operation *Warden* sortie over northern Iraq, the aircraft being unarmed but equipped with a reconnaissance pod. Although Harrier GR 7s routinely carried CBU-87s during such missions, their primary tasking in Operation *Warden* was reconnaissance, monitoring the movement of Iraqi troops in northern Iraq (*Mark Linney*)

This gave extensive photographic coverage of the whole airfield. Off target, we climbed and carried on with the rest of the plan from medium altitude as briefed.

'During the transit home, I began to consider the rules of the Theatre of Operations. The one that bothered me most was that I knew we were not supposed to fly lower than 5000 ft in that target area. The question on my mind was whether or not Command would agree with me that it was better to achieve the mission by improvising and breaking the rules than aborting the target. We would see!

'After landing, we went through the normal routine of signing in the jets and going to the Reconnaissance Intelligence Centre (RIC) to view our camera footage and assist the photographic interpreters (PIs) in orientation, adding pilot reports where appropriate. Upon entering the RIC, I could see that there was clearly some commotion at one of the reviewing tables. A cluster of PIs had gathered and were reviewing our film with some excitement.

'My first thought was the fact they were viewing film from the low-level recce pod, rather than the usual LOROP [Long Range Oblique Photography] film. So I instantly launched into a justification of my decision to run at low-level, perhaps in a defensive tone. The response surprised me. The excitement was more about the imagery than our height. Being at low-level, one of our sideways, oblique-looking cameras had a view inside a hangar on the airfield. The hangar doors were open, and the film revealed imagery of two rows of FROG-7 artillery rockets. These weapons could be used to deliver a selection of warheads, including chemical and nuclear, so were of significant concern. Had we flown the original plan and filmed from medium level, we would not have gathered this imagery. So, in this case, the thunderstorm did us a favour! Apparently, these photos were so important and of such significance they were sent to the Pentagon within minutes.'

The deployment of No 1 Sqn to Turkey proved to be the final Harrier detachment in Operation *Warden*. In April 1995, as tensions built up in the Balkans, the Harrier force handed over responsibility for RAF presence in the northern NFZ to the Tornado GR 1s of No 617 Sqn.

BELIZE

Harrier GR 3s of No 1 Sqn had first deployed to Belize in 1975 when Guatemalan troops were reported massing close to the border with the British dependency. Guatemala had a long-standing claim over the territory of Belize, and it seemed that an invasion was imminent. The deployment of British Army units and supporting Harriers was enough to defuse the immediate threat from Guatemala, and the aircraft were withdrawn from Belize the following year. However, when tensions rose again in June 1977, Harriers were dispatched once more.

The four-aircraft Harrier detachment, later redesignated No 1417 Flight, remained at Belize International Airport for the next 16 years until the threat from Guatemala had diminished sufficiently. During the last of these years, the introduction of the Harrier GR 5 as a replacement for the GR 3 had presented a problem for the Harrier force. The Harrier GR 5 never achieved full combat-ready status, and as such it could not replace the Harrier GR 3. This meant a small number of Harrier GR3s and a cadre of suitably-qualified pilots had to be retained to service the Belize commitment between 1990–93.

Although No 1417 Flight disbanded in July 1993, a Harrier GR 7 deployment to Belize was planned to take place two months later. 'It was a bit of sabre-rattling to show the Guatemalans that we could reinforce Belize pretty quickly', commented Flt Lt Linney. Six Harriers from No 4 Sqn deployed from Laarbruch to Belize, by way of an AAR trail across the Atlantic, to Goose Bay in Labrador. Then, staging down the eastern seaboard of the USA, they arrived in Belize on 8 September.

Flt Lt Al Pinner climbs into the cockpit of a Harrier GR 7 of No 4 Sqn at Belize International Airport in September 1993. A Carrier Bomb Light Stores, which would be loaded with three-kilogram practice bombs for weaponry practice on the New River Lagoon range, is attached to the underwing pylon. During their deployment to Belize, the Harrier pilots of No 4 Sqn also dropped live 1000-lb bombs and fired SNEB rockets (*Andrew Suddards*)

With its tail painted to mark the 80th anniversary of the formation of No 4 Sqn, Harrier GR 7 ZG532, flown by Flt Lt Pat Voigt, flies past the Great Blue Hole off the coast of Belize on 13 September 1993. Two aircraft had been finished in this scheme. Many of the Harrier GR 7 pilots who deployed to Belize in 1993 were familiar with the region, having previously been detached there flying the Harrier GR 3 with No 1417 Flight (*Andrew Suddards*)

During the two weeks that they were in Belize, the Harriers mounted a series of 'flag waving' sorties to advertise their presence both to the Guatemalans and the populace of Belize. 'With Belize being pretty similar in size to Wales', explained Sqn Ldr A J Q Suddards, 'in a one-hour sortie, you could pretty much cover three-quarters if not the whole country, so the recce sortie we undertook on 14 September was about connecting all the interesting places within Belize. Part of what we were doing was reassuring Belize that the Harrier GR 7s could, and would, if necessary, return despite the withdrawal of the GR 3. Hence showing ourselves to the wider population and to the population centres was part of the remit. However, it would have been a severe disappointment not to see the magnificent sites of Belize whilst there, including the famous Great Blue Hole, which has been ranked as number one on the list of "The Ten Most Amazing Places on Earth"'.

Suddards photographed Flt Lt P G O Voigt flying past the Great Blue Hole in a Harrier painted in No 4 Sqn's 80th Anniversary colours on 13 September. Other sorties included live weaponry employment at New River Lagoon weapons range, which saw the dropping of 1,000-lb High Explosive bombs and the firing of SNEB 68 mm rockets.

The squadron personnel changed over halfway through the detachment, with the replacements for the second half arriving by VC10 transport on 15 September. The VC10 was escorted into Belize by four Harriers, which then carried out a simulated attack on the airport. In the second half of the detachment the Harriers also used the New River Lagoon weapons range and carried out a flypast of Belize City for Independence Day on 21 September

The aircraft started their journey back to Germany on 22 September, routing over two days via NAS Key West (in Florida), MCAS Cherry Point (in North Carolina), Loring AFB (in northern Maine) to Goose Bay. Once at the latter airfield, the pilots patiently waited while a small armada of TriStar and VC10K AAR tankers was assembled, along with a Nimrod maritime patrol aircraft to provide search and rescue (SAR) support, for the transatlantic leg. Harriers, tankers and SAR support took off on 27 September. The plan was to drop the Harriers off at Machrihanish, in Scotland, from where they would complete the final leg to Germany the following day. However, favourable tailwinds meant that the tanker formation had sufficient fuel to get at least four of the Harriers back to Laarbruch, and after a final top-up they arrived home after a six-hour flight direct from Goose Bay. Other aircraft and the ground personnel overnighted in Scotland before their return to Germany.

CHAPTER TWO

BOSNIA

OPERATION *DENY FLIGHT*

Soon after the fall of communism in Europe in 1990, ethnic tensions and economic crises triggered the disintegration of the Socialist Federal Republic of Yugoslavia. Nationalist groups within the constituent provinces sought to establish themselves as independent countries and, inevitably, disagreement by other ethnic groups led to violence. The next ten years saw a series of brutal civil wars, amongst the most notorious of which was the Bosnian war which erupted in April 1992. As well as military clashes, this conflict was punctuated by large-scale massacres as the Bosnian Serb Army (BSA) carried out a policy of 'ethnic cleansing.'

NATO had become involved in the Bosnian war in October 1992 when it acted to monitor United Nations Security Council Resolution (UNSCR) 781, which 'establish[ed] a ban on military flights in the airspace of Bosnia and Herzegovina'. Operation *Sky Monitor* was established to check on the observance of the NFZ over Bosnia. It became Operation *Deny Flight* in March 1993 when UNSCR 816 authorised the use of 'all necessary measures' to ensure compliance with the NFZ, and at this stage the RAF dispatched six Tornado F 3s to join the NATO aircraft enforcing the NFZ.

Despite international attempts at mediation, the situation in Bosnia deteriorated further, and in July 1993 nine RAF Jaguars were sent to the Italian air base at Gioia del Colle to provide air support to the United

From the outset, Operation *Vulcan* was a joint effort by the Harrier GR 7s of No 4 Sqn and the Jaguar GR 1Bs of No 6 Sqn. The latter aircraft, which were normally base at Coltishall, used the Ferranti/GEC-Marconi TIALD pod to laser designate targets for the Harriers. Good rapport between the Jaguar and Harrier pilots meant that the mixed formations were very effective. The TIALD pod is clearly visible under the fuselage of the Jaguar in this photograph of a Jaguar/Harrier pair over the Adriatic Sea in September 1995 (*Mark Linney*)

Nations Protection Force (UNPROFOR) on the ground in Bosnia. Four Jaguars, flown by pilots from No 54 Sqn, took part in a NATO air strike on the Serbian Air Force airfield at Udbina on 21 November 1994.

Back in the Britain at about the same time, and largely thanks to the efforts of Sqn Ldr P N Birch, a small number of Jaguars were modified to GR 1B standard, making them capable of using the Ferranti/GEC-Marconi TIALD targeting pod. Three of these aircraft arrived at Gioia del Colle in March 1995 to give the Jaguar force a precision attack capability using Paveway II Laser Guided Bombs (LGBs). Because the Jaguar could not carry both a TIALD pod and an LGB, laser-guided attacks were flown using cooperative designation – in other words, the aircraft worked in pairs with one jet designating the target while the other dropped the bomb.

During the summer of 1995 the BSA seized the UN declared Safe Areas around Gorazde, Zepa and Srebrenica, taking UNPROFOR personnel hostage. With tension mounting in the Balkans, the Harrier GR 7 force prepared to take over responsibility for the offensive support role from the Jaguar force within Operation *Deny Flight*. While No 4 Sqn readied itself to deploy to Gioia del Colle in the summer, pilots from Nos 1 and 3 Sqns had already been practising for another parallel operation.

When British troops were trapped in Gorazde by Bosnian-Serb forces, an operation was planned to extract them by helicopter at night. The helicopters were to be supported by Harriers of Nos 1 and 3 Sqns, which with their new night combat capability would be ideally suited to the task. Sqn Ldr Atha later wrote that the 'key to success would be the intimate synchronisation of Harriers, helicopters and forces on the ground. In preparation, a series of rehearsals were conducted covertly in both Wales and Scotland through 1994 and into early 1995. Aircrew familiarised themselves with every nook and cranny of Gorazde, helped by the creation of a room which had three-dimensional images of the town and surrounding terrain pinned to the walls. However, the plan was overtaken by the events of Operation *Deliberate Force* and the Royal Welch Fusiliers simply drove out of Gorazde'.

The first Harriers from No 4 Sqn began to arrive at Gioia del Colle in late July 1995, and pilots familiarised themselves with the local procedures and the operational area over Bosnia. The first mission, during which Wg Cdr C H Moran and Flt Lt A C Pinner accompanied a Jaguar, was flown on 25 July. By 1 August, 12 GR 7s had relieved the Jaguars of No 6 Sqn. However, at that stage, the TIALD pods had not yet been integrated with and cleared for use on the GR 7, leaving the Harrier force without an indigenous precision attack capability. Instead, the two TIALD-equipped Jaguar GR 1Bs were held on standby at Coltishall, in Norfolk, ready to deploy to Gioia del Colle to act as target designators in the event that the Harriers were called upon to carry out precision guided attacks. One Jaguar remained in theatre until mid-August, and a composite Jaguar–Harrier formation was able to practise the tactics for cooperative laser attacks on 14 August before the Jaguar returned to Coltishall.

Over the summer, the pilots of No 4 Sqn settled into the routine of operations, flying CAS missions for UNPROFOR alternated with training sorties to maintain other skills. Although the aircraft were armed for CAS missions, the Harriers were not called upon to use their weapons in anger.

The concept was to keep an armed presence over the UNPROFOR contingents at this stage. Launching in pairs throughout the day, the Harriers would be allocated to a Forward Air Controller (FAC) with an UNPROFOR unit. They would then set up a holding pattern overhead and make dummy attacks on various targets chosen by the FAC.

In addition to these predominantly medium-level flights, reconnaissance sorties using the Vinten pod photographed BSA military facilities. Although AAR support was available from RAF TriStars based at Ancona, the Harrier GR 7s flying from Gioia del Colle usually had enough range to operate over Bosnia without the need to refuel routinely. Other training sorties included bombing a splash target towed by the Type 42 destroyer HMS *Nottingham* in the Adriatic Sea, as well as two-versus-two Dissimilar Air Combat Training against *Armée de l'Air* Mirage 2000s and Dutch F-16s.

Meanwhile, reports of the massacre of some 7000–8000 Muslim men by the BSA at Srebrenica and Zepa in mid-July began to emerge as international attempts to bring the war to a close continued. The peace process was further frustrated by a mortar attack by the BSA on a marketplace in Sarajevo that killed 38 civilians on 29 August, and led UN/NATO commanders to believe that an attack on Sarajevo was imminent. This was the catalyst for NATO to launch military action against Serbian forces involving artillery bombardment by the NATO Multi-National Brigade (MN Bde) and air strikes by NATO aircraft. This armed action, codenamed Operation *Deliberate Force*, was intended to neutralise BSA heavy weapons near Sarajevo and disable the BSA command and control structure, thereby inhibiting the army's ability to manoeuvre rapidly across the region.

The MN Bde had commenced its artillery attack on BSA positions near Sarajevo on 28 August, and offensive action by NATO aircraft against the

Armourers check 1000-lb Paveway II LGBs to ensure that they are ready for loading on to a Harrier GR 7 at Gioia del Colle. Typically, a Harrier would be loaded with two such weapons for an Operation *Vulcan* mission. During the short campaign over Bosnia-Herzegovina, Harrier GR 7s dropped 48 Paveway IIs on 19 targets (*Crown Copyright/MoD*)

An LGB-armed Harrier GR 7 is accompanied by TIALD-equipped Jaguar GR 1B XX748 during an Operation *Vulcan* sortie. Both aircraft are also armed with AIM-9L Sidewinders. Typically, one Jaguar would work with a pair of Harriers, designating targets for each aircraft in turn. Although the weather over the Balkans was rarely as clear as this, making accurate laser-designation of targets difficult to achieve, it was reckoned the combined Jaguar/Harrier attacks achieved a success rate of more than 80 per cent (*Andrew Suddards*)

command-and-control structures started two days later. As the personnel in the Harrier detachment at Gioia del Colle readied themselves for action, the Jaguar GR 1B pilots at Coltishall waited for the order to deploy. 'The call came late on the afternoon of 29 August', wrote Sqn Ldr A J Muskett of No 6 Sqn. 'Only one aircraft was ready, so I departed Coltishall at around 1700 hrs and, having refuelled in Nice, arrived at Gioia del Colle that evening at around 2100 hrs. "Blakey" [Flt Lt S Blake] was to follow me the following morning and, on his arrival, was thrown straight into planning for an operational sortie that same afternoon'.

Flt Lt Blake later recalled that he 'had been on leave for most of August. On return to work, I spent 24–25 August regaining TIALD currency which proved insightful. After the Sarajevo bombing, it became clear that NATO was going to react. On 29 August, I was tasked to take a jet and pod to Boscombe Down for a harmonisation, as we did not have the facility at Coltishall. That took most of the day, and I had to fly back very late that same evening with a temporary canopy seal repair (a Bic biro!) that ended up lasting the next few weeks. I had enough time to get home, pack a bag and then get up early on 30 August to meet a VC10K out of Brize Norton, which tanked me to the French FIR [flight information region] boundary, at which point I reckoned I had enough fuel to get direct to Gioia. I landed straight into the [operational] plan[ning].'

The British participation in the air strikes, codenamed Operation *Vulcan*, started on 30 August with two waves of attacks against the ammunition storage facility at Hadzici and the BSA headquarters at Pale. Both of these targets were large arrays consisting of around 20 individual bunkers or buildings, each of which constituted a separate target with a specific aiming point. In the case of Hadzici, there were also two other target sites in close proximity – a military vehicle repair facility and a military equipment storage site. Target acquisition would therefore be complicated.

The Harriers formed part of five large strike packages mounted throughout the day, designated Alpha to Echo, which included Suppression of Enemy Air Defence (SEAD) assets and fighter escort for the strike aircraft. The first RAF formation to launch, as part of Strike Package Charlie, was a six-ship comprising two Jaguars each leading two Harriers, tasked against Hadzici. In the first section, Sqn Ldr Muskett accompanied Sqn Ldr Suddards and Flt Lt R Holmes, while in the second, Flt Lt Blake was the target designator for Flt Lts Linney and Voigt. The Jaguars were equipped with TIALD pods and each Harrier was armed with two Paveway II 1000-lb LGBs.

'Our Standard Operating Procedure was for the Jaguar to effectively lead and the GR 7 guys to act as lookouts, using their ARBS as a situational awareness tool', recalled Blake. 'This proved very effective, and allowed us to stay "heads in" [the cockpit] a lot. This was necessary as the Jaguar had no auto pilot or height/heading hold. Thus, we acquired the target and then lased, with the GR 7 guys confirming a good "spot" and also helping with finessing the track (which on occasion proved very helpful)'.

Sqn Ldr Suddards commented further that 'if the Jags were firing their lasers, we could put our TV in scan mode and, with the same codes entered, we could confirm that the Jags were lasing the correct target. We used verbal confirmation codewords too, such as "Six seconds", "Three seconds" to bomb release, with the Jags confirming "Happy" or "No Joy". Our weapon aiming system had auto release on TV or laser lock, which gave us the timing countdown. So, we were pretty well placed to have double confirmation – verbal from the Jags and what we were seeing on our screens to know that the right target was being lased'.

Over Bosnia, the combined formation encountered intermittent layers of low cloud, and on reaching the vicinity of Hadzici, Muskett in the lead Jaguar could see that the target itself was obscured by banks of broken cloud. 'I was unable to identify my target on the first pass', he admitted, 'so I was forced into a re-attack, allowing "Blakey" and his pair to sneak in ahead, and so become the first single-seat RAF pilot to prosecute an attack using an airborne laser-designator on operations'.

Following just two minutes behind the first section, Blake found that the cloud had moved sufficiently to allow him a clear view of the target, and give Linney and Voigt the opportunity to drop their weapons successfully. Muskett, too, was able to acquire the target on his second pass, allowing Suddards and Holmes to also deliver their bombs accurately. It was with some irony that the three Qualified Flying Instructors dropped the first bombs of the campaign, rather than the three QWIs in the first section.

The attack had been a complete success, and as Sqn Ldr Suddards pointed out, 'being one of the first sorties and first buddy lasing efforts, we were delighted that things seemed to work well. The Jag was able to operate in a cleaner, lighter fit, and therefore had good medium-level performance. The Harrier had better inherent medium level performance, and easily coped with the extra weight and drag of the bombs'.

However, the mission was not yet over, and a challenge still remained for the six pilots in the shape of a large thunderstorm over Gioia del

Colle. 'The weather was atrocious', recalled Flt Lt Linney. 'When I was two or three miles out on approach, I was still unable to see the runway. I had designated the touchdown point as a "target", the position of which was being projected in the head-up display [HUD], but all that was pointing at was a very dark evil-looking thunder cloud! I had nowhere else to go, nor any scope to hold off because I had no fuel left!

'I was literally looking out either side of the cockpit for a road to land on, and I was about to take up that option – something you can consider in a Harrier in an emergency – when I eventually saw the outline of the runway. I carried out a rolling vertical landing with a groundspeed of about 50 knots on what was a flooded surface in torrential rain with very poor visibility. The groundcrew came out to greet us as we taxied in and their jaws dropped for two reasons. Firstly, that we were even there, because for some time they had been sheltering from a violent thunderstorm, and secondly, because we didn't have any bombs under our wings! For many of our groundcrew this was their first experience of combat operations, and in that moment, things got real for them too.'

The second Harrier wave on 30 August was part of Strike Package Delta (the fourth of the large multi-national air strikes), for which Sqn Ldr Atha was the overall package commander. He also flew on the mission, with Maj Hile on his wing, and was supported by Sqn Ldr Muskett flying his second sortie of the day in the Jaguar.

'Strike Package Delta involved 24 British, French and American aircraft tasked with attacking targets surrounding Pale, a Bosnian Serb stronghold', explained Atha. 'The sortie had not started well, with both my wingman's, then my aircraft developing faults, which delayed mission launch. Although this involved swapping precision bombs for dumb bombs, it was decided that Muskett would continue to support the mission by using the Jaguar laser to help us locate and attack our targets.

'Despite the delayed launch, the mission proceeded because the attack plan included enough time over target to allow any late comers from Strike Package Delta to flow in at the end of the bracket. This meant that the RAF formation would be the "tail end Charlies" of the mission – never the safest place to be in any attack. The new order of arrival over the target was, therefore, Americans, French and then the British. The weather over Bosnia was not great, with a general cloud base of around 12,000 ft, which

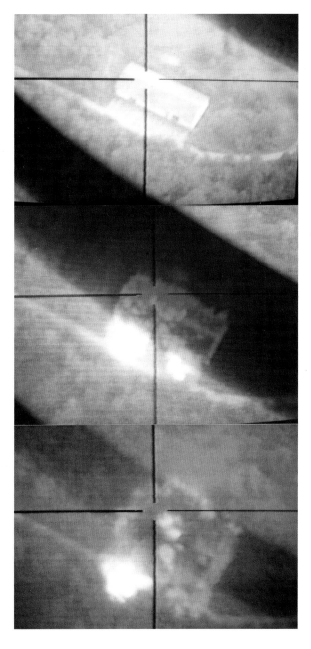

A Serbian ammunition storage building at Hadzici is struck by a bomb dropped by a Harrier GR 7 during the first attack of Operation *Vulcan*. This was typical of many of the targets attacked during the campaign – storage sites tended to comprise a number of small buildings dispersed within a relatively large target area. In marginal weather, target acquisition could be challenging (*Mark Linney*)

dropped even lower where there were showers. To identify targets, aircraft were forced to fly within range of Serbian missile and gun systems.

'After a challenging descent through cloud, we transited across Bosnia, passed Sarajevo and joined the tail of Strike Package Delta. As we approached the target area near the Serbian stronghold of Pale, the scene was reminiscent of World War 2 footage. Plumes of smoke billowed into the air and many of the ammunition storage buildings and factories surrounding the town were already ablaze, with flames leaping high into the sky.

'"Musky" fired his laser at the designated target, helping me lock the Harrier GR 7's Dual Mode Tracking system onto the ammunition storage shed. With seconds to go, my thumb was hovering above the control column, ready to press the bright red circular bomb release button, when Hile spotted the launch of two missiles from a spot high up on the side of Mount Igman, northwest of the target area. Responding to Hile's warning call, I aggressively manoeuvred my aircraft and dispensed flares – the ingrained response drilled into all Harrier pilots.

'As I threw my aircraft round the sky, I looked over my shoulder to see, disappointingly, the upwards expanding smoke trail of two SAMs continuing to arc towards me. Readying myself for the well-practiced Harrier end game manoeuvre, which involves the pilot conducting a violent barrel roll around the missile to generate sufficient miss distance to survive, both missiles, rather disconcertingly, disappeared. The end of the smoke trail marked the end of the rocket-assisted boost phase of the launch, but not the end of the missile's flight. This had not been mentioned in the tactics manual – how do you fight a missile you cannot see? After a tense couple of seconds the missiles thankfully reappeared as they automatically detonated some 2000 ft from the aircraft.

'Despite the shock of the missile launch and the descent to low altitude over Mount Igman during the manoeuvres to defeat the SAMs, Hile and I reformed formation and re-attacked the target from a different direction. In the mayhem during the missile launch, Muskett had very sensibly continued to fly his Jaguar south of the target, and the time remaining prevented him re-joining the formation. The re-attack had mixed success, with Hile successfully destroying his target. I, however, could not release my bombs because of a wiring problem in the underwing pylon, which had a whiff of irony given that I could have jettisoned my bombs during the manoeuvres to defeat the Serbian missiles.

'Unlucky as this might be, the French crew of a Mirage 2000 in Strike Package Delta were much less fortunate. Flying ahead of the Harriers, they had not spotted the Serbian missile fired at them as they attacked the target. Both aircrew, Capt Frederic Chiffot and Lt Jose Souvignet, survived the shootdown, and the pot-shots taken at them as they floated down in their parachutes. Quickly taken prisoner, they endured an extended period of incarceration by the Serbs until they were released four months later. Capt Chiffot and I met again some 15 years later in Paris, where we discovered that we had both been attacked by missiles fired from the same location on Mount Igman. Chiffot revealed that he and Souvignet had broken legs on landing and subsequently been the subject of brutal physical and psychological torture through their period in captivity.

'The RAF Harrier force benefited much from its links with its cousins in the US Marine Corps. On this occasion, it was thanks to the eagle-eyed look out of Maj Mike Hile that I had not joined Capt Chiffot and Lt Souvignet as a Prisoner of War, or worse.'

For his part, Maj Hile (a 70+ mission veteran of Operation *Desert Storm* in 1991) noted 'that sortie was unforgettable. And after that mission, I felt like I had earned my spot as a pilot among the RAF'.

The next day, 31 August, brought more of the poor weather which would hamper much of the campaign, with layered cloud across most of Serbia and Kosovo and fog covering much of the terrain. The events of the day also highlighted the delicate reliability of the early TIALD pods, which would also cause problems. The two TIALD Jaguars launched from Gioia del Colle, each leading a pair of Harriers to bomb an ammunition storage area at Ustikolina. Unfortunately, Muskett suffered a TIALD pod failure soon after take-off and returned to base, leaving Blake to cover the targets for both pairs of Harriers. However, the mission had to be aborted when it became clear that the weather over Bosnia was unsuitable, forcing all aircraft to return with their weapons on board.

That evening, Gen Bernard Janvier, the commander of UN forces in Bosnia, ordered the bombing to be ceased initially for 24 hours (and later extended to four days) while negotiations were held with the Bosnian Serb leader Gen Ratko Mladic. However, Harrier operations continued over the next few days, with reconnaissance missions flown over Bosnia.

Pairs of Harriers patrolled the area at medium-level, using the Vinten pod to monitor the movements and location of BSA troops, and to check activity at Serbian barracks and military depots. When negotiations between Janvier and Mladic came to nothing, offensive action was resumed at 1305 hrs on 5 September. That afternoon, Wg Cdr C H Moran (OC No 4 Sqn) led Sqn Ldr Atha and Flt Lt J D Provost, supported by Sqn Ldr Muskett, against the ammunition depot at Ustikolina, once again in marginal weather.

As they approached the target area, the aircraft came under fire from AAA, but it was actually the low clouds that prevented Muskett from finding the target with the TIALD pod, causing the mission to be aborted. Flt Lt Blake was luckier with the weather conditions 30 miles further to the east, and he was able to designate ammunition storage bunkers at Visegrad for Flt Lts I Cameron and S Ashworth, who scored direct hits. 'One hit was spectacular, and the building had clearly contained some other ordnance', commented Blake. A second attempt against Ustikolina the following day, this time involving AAR support, was once again thwarted by the weather over the target area. So, too, was a follow-up operation against Visegrad.

The first target on 7 September was the radio relay station at Doboj, with two Jaguar–Harrier pairs tasked for the mission. This time it was Flt Lt Blake who suffered a TIALD pod failure and Sqn Ldr Muskett 'spiked' for both Harriers. However, difficulty in acquiring the correct aiming point in an area that had already been heavily attacked meant that the bombs dropped by Wg Cdr Moran and Flt Lt Provost all missed the target.

On his second sortie of the day, Muskett marked the Visegrad ammunition storage bunkers for two Harrier GR 7s flown by Sqn Ldrs

Atha and S C Meade. Each Harrier dropped two LGBs, and this time both pilots scored direct hits on their targets. After supporting this successful attack, Muskett refuelled from an RAF TriStar AAR tanker before returning to the operational area to rendezvous with four more Harriers for an attack on an electronic warfare (EW) deployment site at Tuzla.

Sqn Ldr Suddards later remembered the target as being 'a typical AAA site with several guns emplacements, and a radar emplacement that had horseshoe earth berms built around the equipment piece'. LGBs dropped by the first pair of Harrier GR 7s flown by Sqn Ldr Suddards and Maj Hile caused severe damage to the target, which was finally destroyed by the second pair comprising Flt Lts D Haines and J Hatton-Ward. Muskett returned to Gioia del Colle after a 3 hr 40 min flight.

That same day, four Harrier GR 7s flown by Flt Lts Cameron, Ashworth, Linney and Voigt struck another EW site at Nevesinje, which was defended by a S-60 AAA battery. With no Jaguar available to mark the target for an LGB attack, each of the aircraft were instead loaded with two 1000-lb freefall bombs. They were delivered in a 30-degree diving attack into the 'face' of the S-60 emplacement.

Flt Lt Linney later commented, 'it was noteworthy because just as I was coming up to weapon release I could see that they were shooting at me. I was going down in the dive, getting everything lined up, when I saw the muzzle flashes coming from exactly where I was aiming. I thought to myself, "hang on a minute, they're actually shooting at me!", so I released my weapons. As I recovered from the dive, I said to myself "that wasn't very friendly of them!" I didn't see the flak, as I was too pre-occupied at the time, but I'm fairly sure I came off the better in that exchange'.

Armed reconnaissance sorties were also launched in parallel to the strike missions. On 8 September Wg Cdr Moran led Flt Lt Linney on a 2 hr 40 min sortie which was supported by a USAF KC-10 tanker. Yet again they incurred the wrath of the test pilots at Boscombe Down, who had not yet cleared the Harrier to use the American tanker! Flt Lt Linney commented afterwards, 'the KC-10 was there, and we needed fuel. It wasn't in the Release to Service document, but we only discovered this after the event'. Thereafter, using the KC-10 was not an uncommon occurrence.

In the early afternoon, another reconnaissance mission was reroled by the strike controller aboard the Airborne Battlefield Command and Control Center aircraft to attack an interdiction target. Although the Harriers were cleared to drop their weapons, the target that they were tasked against was close to a detachment of Russian peacekeeping troops who were somewhat surprised by the arrival of bombs close to their position.

Flt Lt Mark 'Dins' Linney in the cockpit of a Harrier GR 7 at Gioia del Colle during Operation *Vulcan*. Note the white bomb symbols (six for LGBs and four for freefall bombs) painted below the cockpit, each representing a sortie on which weapons were expended (Mark Linney)

As well as LGB operations, Harrier GR 7s dropped freefall 1000-lb bombs during the Bosnia conflict and also carried out patrols armed with CBU-87 cluster bombs. An example of the latter weapon is seen in this close-up view of a Harrier during an Operation *Vulcan* mission (*Mark Linney*)

That same day, Flt Lts Cameron and Ashworth and Sqn Ldr Atha were tasked with Flt Lt Blake in the TIALD Jaguar against a target in Jahorina, some 12 miles southeast of Sarajevo. Once again, the mission was abandoned because of a combination of clouds partially obscuring the target and, ultimately, a TIALD pod failure.

A radio relay station at Tuzla proved to be an elusive target during Operation *Deliberate Force*, despite the attention of both Harriers and French Mirage 2000s. According to Sqn Ldr Atha, 'a friendly rivalry had grown between the French and British squadrons. This was best exemplified by a "race" to be first to destroy an important and particularly large communications mast north of Tuzla – a mission that became known as "Operation Timber". Both nations had made a number of attempts, but had been thwarted by the weather'.

Two attempts by No 4 Sqn to bomb the mast on 9 September were abandoned because the target was obscured by clouds, and the first mission the following day was aborted when Flt Lt Blake experienced fumes in the cockpit of his Jaguar. Later, on 10 September, Flt Lts Pinner and Hatton-Ward set out for a second attempt against the mast, accompanied by Sqn Ldr Muskett in the TIALD Jaguar. When they arrived in the target area, the formation was re-tasked to a CAS target, but this proved too difficult to locate with the TIALD pod. After refuelling from a TriStar AAR tanker, the three aircraft returned to Tuzla and attack their original target. Here, they were joined by Wg Cdr Moran, Sqn Ldr Suddards and Maj Hile, each carrying two 1000-lb freefall bombs.

Sqn Ldr Suddards commented that it was 'a significant effort to take down what was a very large radar and comms relay site sitting atop a high hill. It was a large brick/concrete tower with a weather covered radome on top. We were using primarily our TV ARBS to identify and edge lock onto the targets, with straight and level auto weapons release. So long as the TV stayed locked to the target, it was just a matter of holding the button down to accept the release and the bombs came off when the weapon aiming computer decided. Whilst not "precision bombing" in the sense that the bombs were guided, the accuracy was extremely impressive at around 50–70 ft Circular Error Probable – extremely suitable to such a site, where there was no risk of collateral damage. There was a lot of firepower for the one target, and given the clear weather that allowed ease of identification of such a large target, the attack was both relatively straightforward and impressive at the same time'.

With dusk fast approaching, the five Harriers carried out an almost simultaneous attack on the site. 'Unsurprisingly', recorded Sqn Ldr Atha, 'the mast was successfully downed, and as the squadron aircraft also carried reconnaissance pods, a photograph of it laying on the ground was taken and subsequently sent to the French detachment, declaring "Operation Timber" complete'. The Harriers landed in the dark after sorties of more than three-and-a-half hours.

The next morning (11 September) it was the turn of Flt Lt Blake to lead the first mission of the day in the TIALD Jaguar, but the sortie had to be abandoned because there was no SEAD support available. On his second mission, Blake was the designator for four Harrier GR 7s flown by Flt Lts Ashworth, Cameron, Linney and Voigt, each carrying LGBs for an attack on the Hadzici ammunition depot. Four different buildings within the depot complex had been selected as targets for the four Harriers. Unfortunately, the wrong building was marked for Linney to bomb, but he nevertheless scored a direct hit on it with one of his LGBs. The other bomb did not guide (one of the hazards of using LGBs), and it landed in open countryside approximately two miles short of the target.

For his third mission of the day, Blake was joined by Sqn Ldr Muskett as they led four Harriers against ammunition storage bunkers at Ustikolina. During this attack, Muskett carried out two 'spiking' runs against targets for one of the Harriers, which dropped a single LGB on each pass. Meanwhile, Blake marked the targets for Maj Hile and Flt Lt Hatton-Ward, but he experienced some problems with his TIALD pod. As he explained, the laser 'spot kept moving. Maj Hile talked me back on as the bomb was already falling, and the Paveway II had just about enough energy to "knock on the door" before hitting it!' Blake recorded another direct hit, albeit a lucky one.

The Hadzici ammunition depot, which was by now becoming a familiar target, was attacked again on 12 September. Wg Cdr Moran dropped two LGBs on a hardened bunker, but Muskett lost tracking with his TIALD pod, which then failed, and both bombs fell short. In the second Jaguar, Blake was marking a storage bunker for Flt Lt Hatton-Ward. 'This target was weaponeered with experts from the MoD', explained Blake. 'The result was the correct fusing to penetrate the bunker and just blow the doors out, leaving a puff of smoke from the rear ventilation shaft. Very satisfying!' He continued, 'the whole detachment was a great success, and became known as the "Italian Job" – with some obvious references from the film acting as

The officers and aircrew of No 4 Sqn (Harrier) and No 6 Sqn (Jaguar) who took part in Operation *Vulcan*, photographed after hostilities had ceased. Their aircraft, in appropriate weapons configuration, make an impressive backdrop. The Harrier GR 7s of No 4 Sqn flew 144 daylight combat missions during the campaign (*Mark Linney*)

part of a soundtrack to a very cheesy video that was put together, including the "blowing the doors off" from this sortie'.

The attack on Hadzici was the last successful 'live' mission of Operation *Vulcan*. The following day, 13 September, another attack on the Ustikolina ammunition depot by four Harriers and two Jaguars was aborted because of the weather conditions. A ceasefire came into effect on 14 September. During the two weeks of the operation, the Harriers had flown 144 daylight combat missions and dropped 48 LGBs against 19 targets. A further 30 free-fall bombs were expended on eight more targets. 'I recall that we calculated at the time that in excess of 80 per cent of attacks were successful, with the odd failure primarily due to faults with the TIALD pod', Muskett recalled.

The bombing had come to an end, but reconnaissance and armed overwatch sorties continued through the next few days. On 16 September, Sqn Ldr Atha led Wg Cdr Moran, Flt Lt Linney and Sqn Ldr Meade on a road reconnaissance mission, looking for the movement of BSA heavy weapons – with the end of the bombing campaign, air operations over Bosnia returned to the routine of reconnaissance and CAS support for UNPROFOR. The Jaguars were no longer required in-theatre, and they returned to Coltishall, via Istres, on 25 September.

Operation *Deliberate Force* had been a great success. Decisive action had brought the BSA to heel, paving the way for the Dayton Accords that were signed two months later, bringing an end to hostilities in Bosnia-Herzegovina.

Operation *Vulcan*, too, was an outstanding success for the Harrier GR 7 force, which had achieved its aim and shown its impressive capability, despite difficult and challenging conditions. Flt Lt Linney probably spoke for the whole Harrier detachment when he stated that 'we felt this was a worthy thing, trying to limit the military capabilities of the Serbians who were killing innocent people'. And Maj Hile 'also learned about the humanity of war while with the RAF. An example of this was when we were assigned a target that turned out to be a 1000-year-old bridge – an historic landmark. When assigned by CAOC [Combined Air Operations Centre], No 4 Sqn requested a target reassignment. I am not sure that a US unit would have had the same inclination'.

With hostilities over, the routine of supporting UNPROFOR troops was extended to include reconnaissance sorties searching for evidence of BSA 'ethnic cleansing'. Sqn Ldr S C Turner, formerly of No 1 Sqn and now a staff pilot with No 20 Sqn (the Harrier Operational Conversion Unit), who deployed to Gioia del Colle in June 1996, described how 'for the recce task we carried a variety of pods with a mix of cameras. Our targets were mostly alleged positions of mass graves from Serbian genocidal activities. These sites would be quite visible as newly disturbed ground on our camera imagery. The imagery would be examined by our PIs and sent for further investigation if suspected of being viable.

'We used oblique-looking medium altitude cameras that required a very accurate track to be flown in order to capture target imagery. This required accurate planning using prior knowledge of a specific target area and accurate flying of the profile in order to capture the imagery of the right positions. We typically flew profiles from around 10,000–18,000 ft above target level, with the target offset to the left side by about five miles. The pilot had to maintain a very accurate track over the ground, with the aircraft's wings being precisely level.

'Line of site to the target was essential, so any cloud formation between the aircraft and the target would mean a complicated airborne re-plan to ensure imagery was gathered. Without the Harrier Nav System and displays, this task would otherwise have involved an extremely high workload, but as usual with the Harrier force, we liked a challenge. So, when something became easier, we accepted more work. Consequently, a typical recce mission in this theatre would include numerous targets – sometimes between 20 to 30 recce targets were commonly tasked. This presented many challenges, not least of which was managing the amount of film used on each target, organising routing between targets, creating maps of each target to cross-check geographical position for accurate target coverage, sorting maps in a small cockpit and keeping track of visual observations. All this had to be done in parallel with provision of mutual support and lookout in a threat environment.'

Turner was also impressed with the seamless inter-operability between NATO air forces. On the night of 19 June 1996, he was flying in a pair flying a CAS mission over Sarajevo when, 'around midnight, we reached our fuel minimum and departed to a tanker area. Arriving in the tanker box over the Adriatic, our job was to find the tanker, which was easily achieved using NVGs to locate a very well illuminated tanker aircraft. And with no knowledge of which tanker was on station (it turned out to be a Spanish KC-130 Hercules), we arrived, refuelled to full and departed back to conduct more CAS. This air-to-air refuelling was all achieved using only visual signals without any radio calls'.

Each Harrier squadron took its turn to staff the detachment at Gioia del Colle for a three-month period, until February 1997, when No 3 Sqn handed responsibility for Operation *Deliberate Guard* back to the Jaguars of No 41 Sqn. (*text continues on page 48*)

33

COLOUR PLATES

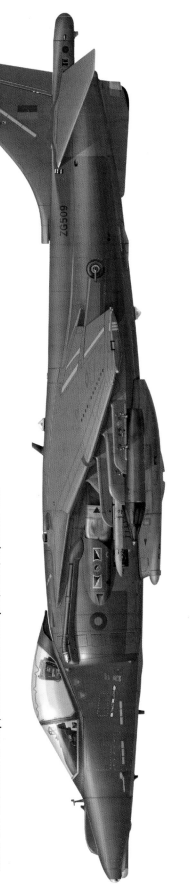

1
Harrier GR 7 ZG509/CH of No 4 Sqn, Belize International Airport, Belize, September 1993

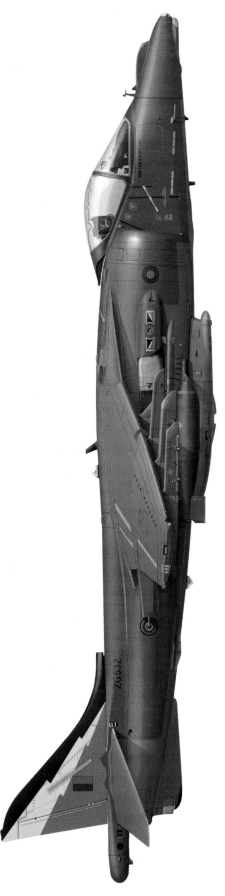

2
Harrier GR 7 ZG532 of No 4 Sqn, Belize International Airport, Belize, September 1993

34

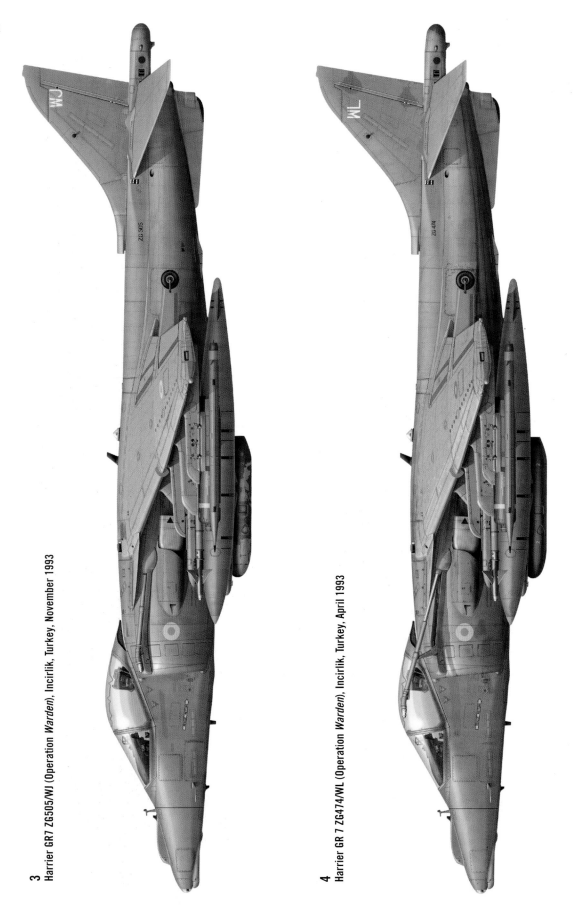

3
Harrier GR7 ZG505/WJ (Operation *Warden*), Incirlik, Turkey, November 1993

4
Harrier GR 7 ZG474/WL (Operation *Warden*), Incirlik, Turkey, April 1993

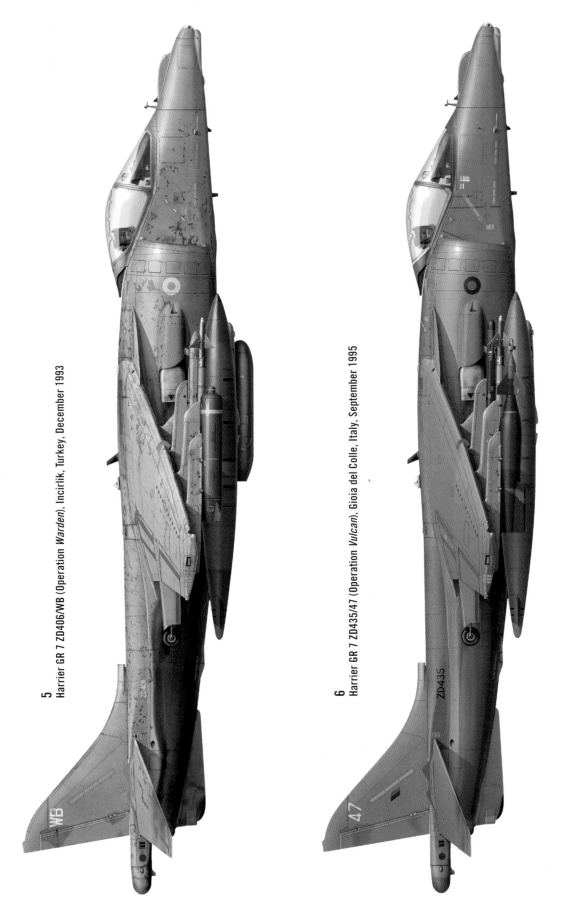

5
Harrier GR 7 ZD406/WB (Operation *Warden*), Incirlik, Turkey, December 1993

6
Harrier GR 7 ZD435/47 (Operation *Vulcan*), Gioia del Colle, Italy, September 1995

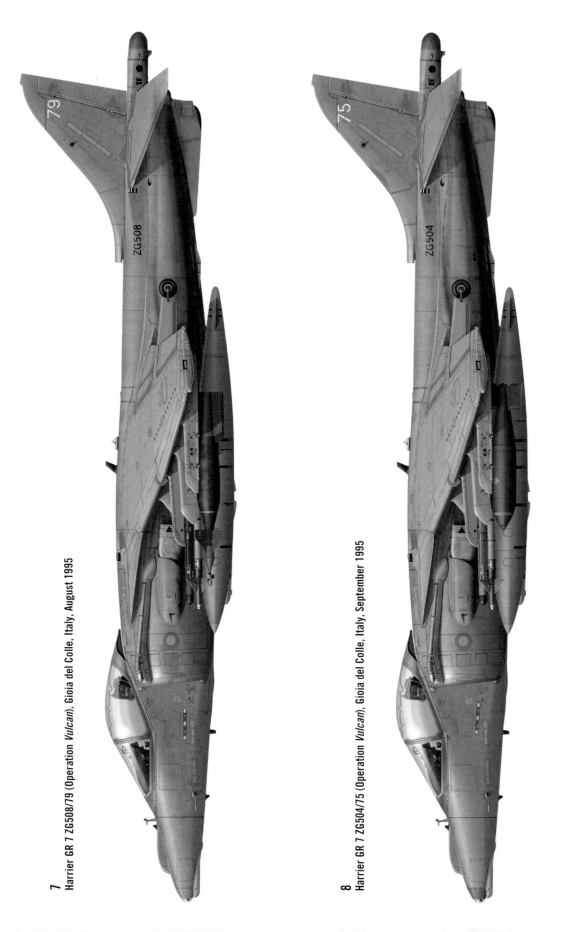

7
Harrier GR 7 ZG508/79 (Operation *Vulcan*), Gioia del Colle, Italy, August 1995

8
Harrier GR 7 ZG504/75 (Operation *Vulcan*), Gioia del Colle, Italy, September 1995

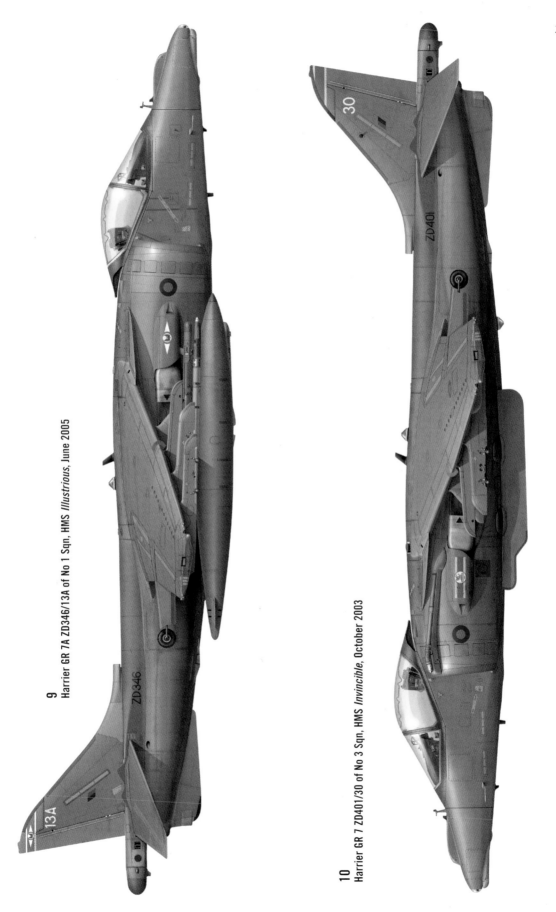

9
Harrier GR 7A ZD346/13A of No 1 Sqn, HMS *Illustrious*, June 2005

10
Harrier GR 7 ZD401/30 of No 3 Sqn, HMS *Invincible*, October 2003

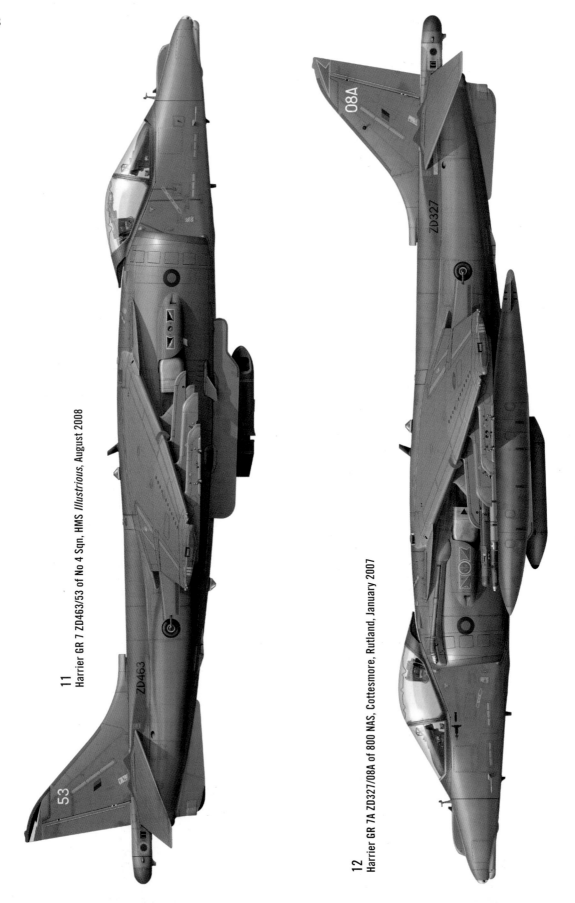

11
Harrier GR 7 ZD463/53 of No 4 Sqn, HMS *Illustrious*, August 2008

12
Harrier GR 7A ZD327/08A of 800 NAS, Cottesmore, Rutland, January 2007

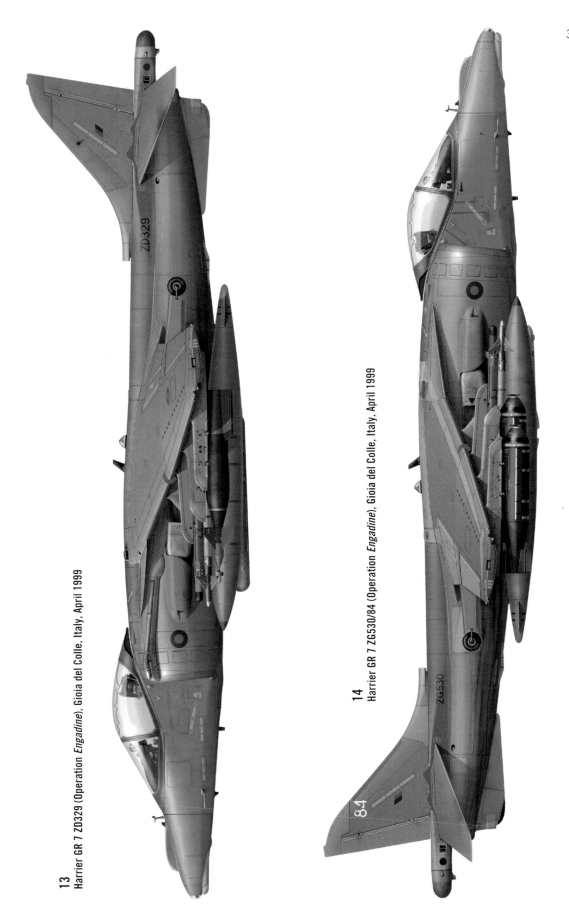

13
Harrier GR 7 ZD329 (Operation *Engadine*), Gioia del Colle, Italy, April 1999

14
Harrier GR 7 ZG530/84 (Operation *Engadine*), Gioia del Colle, Italy, April 1999

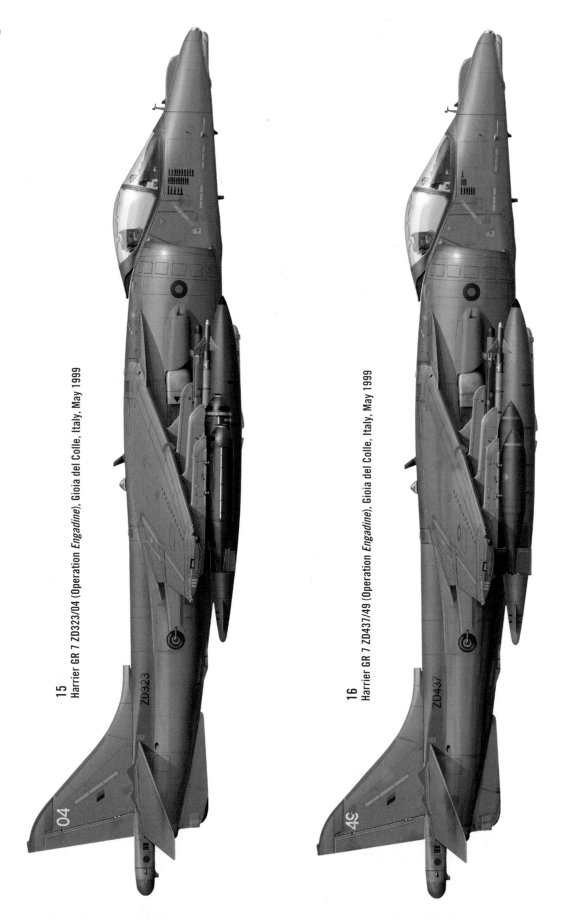

15
Harrier GR 7 ZD323/04 (Operation *Engadine*), Gioia del Colle, Italy, May 1999

16
Harrier GR 7 ZD437/49 (Operation *Engadine*), Gioia del Colle, Italy, May 1999

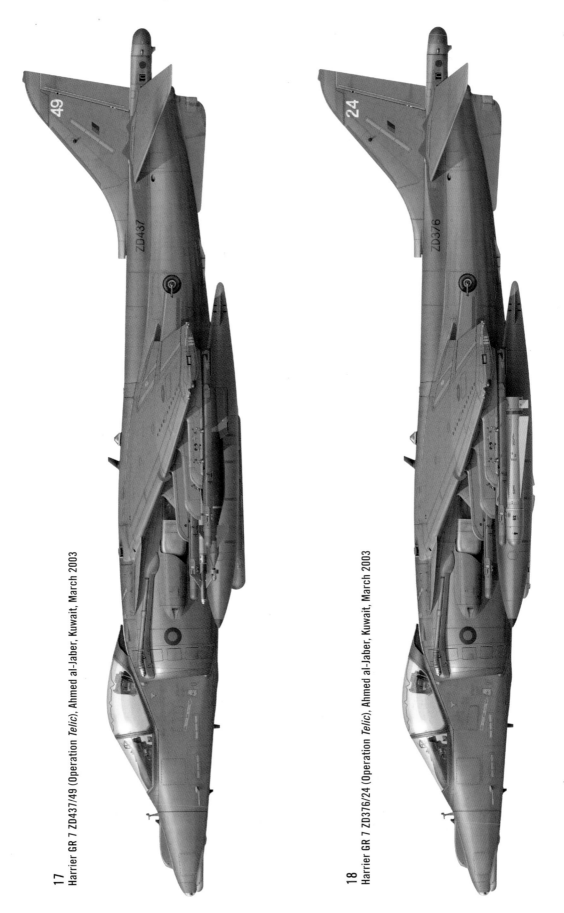

17
Harrier GR 7 ZD437/49 (Operation *Telic*), Ahmed al-Jaber, Kuwait, March 2003

18
Harrier GR 7 ZD376/24 (Operation *Telic*), Ahmed al-Jaber, Kuwait, March 2003

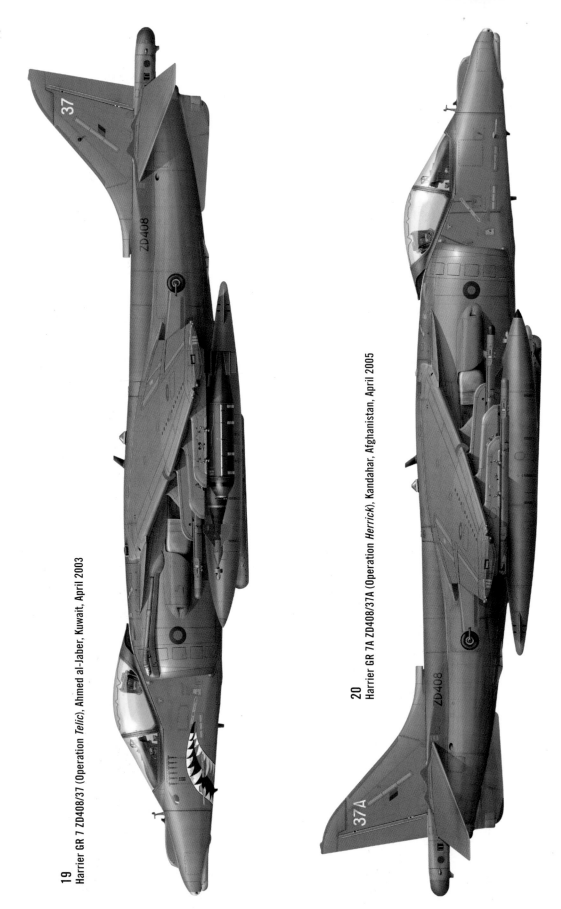

19
Harrier GR 7 ZD408/37 (Operation *Telic*), Ahmed al-Jaber, Kuwait, April 2003

20
Harrier GR 7A ZD408/37A (Operation *Herrick*), Kandahar, Afghanistan, April 2005

43

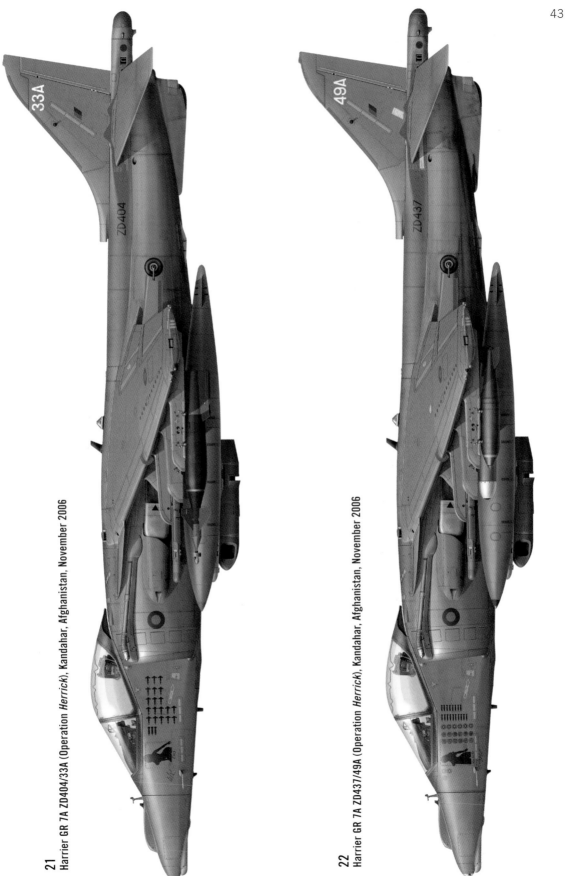

21
Harrier GR 7A ZD404/33A (Operation *Herrick*), Kandahar, Afghanistan, November 2006

22
Harrier GR 7A ZD437/49A (Operation *Herrick*), Kandahar, Afghanistan, November 2006

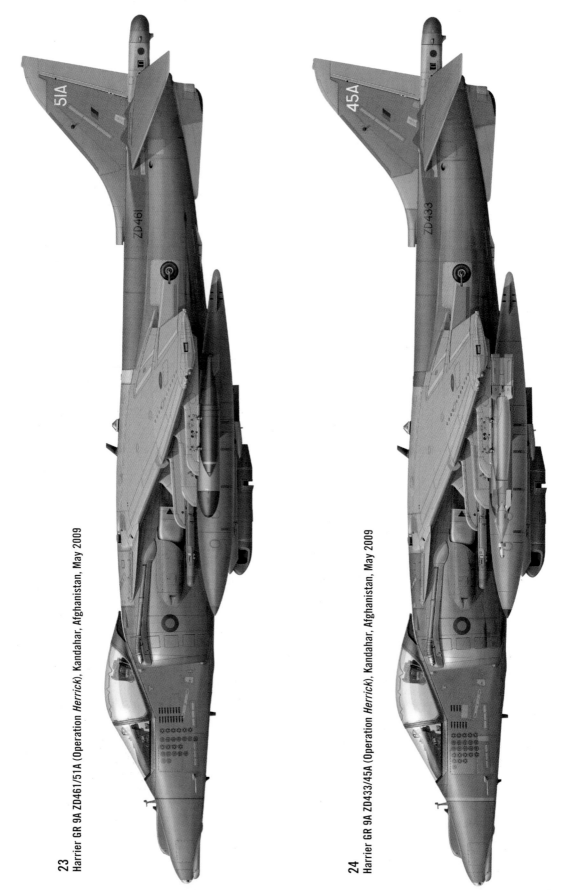

23
Harrier GR 9A ZD461/51A (Operation *Herrick*), Kandahar, Afghanistan, May 2009

24
Harrier GR 9A ZD433/45A (Operation *Herrick*), Kandahar, Afghanistan, May 2009

UNIT BADGES AND NOSE ART

2
Harrier GR 7 ZG532 of No 4 Sqn, Belize International Airport, Belize, September 1993

9
Harrier GR 7A ZD346/13A of No 1 Sqn, HMS *Illustrious*, June 2005

46

10
Harrier GR 7 ZD401/30 of No 3 Sqn, HMS *Invincible*, October 2003

12
Harrier GR 7A ZD327/08A of 800 NAS, Cottesmore, Rutland, January 2007

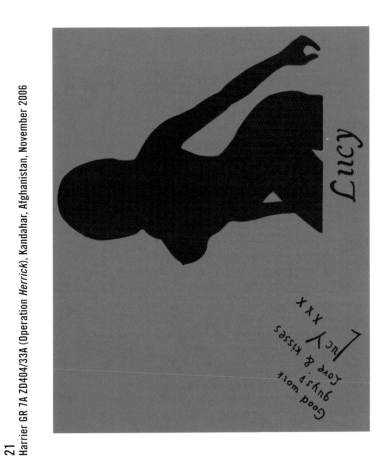

21
Harrier GR 7A ZD404/33A (Operation *Herrick*), Kandahar, Afghanistan, November 2006

22
Harrier GR 7A ZD437/49A (Operation *Herrick*), Kandahar, Afghanistan, November 2006

CARRIER OPERATIONS

Since the Falklands conflict of 1982, when Harrier GR 3s of No 1 Sqn had flown into combat from HMS *Hermes*, the RAF Harrier force had continued to practise operating from Royal Navy aircraft carriers (CVS) on an occasional basis. After the Harrier GR 7 was introduced to service, trials for the new variant to operate from the CVS were carried out successfully in 1994. Three years later, the decision was taken that all frontline Harrier GR 7 units should be capable of CVS operations on a more permanent basis. Pilots were to carry out a 'CVS work-up' syllabus of five sorties to familiarise themselves with the techniques for CVS operations, after which they were fully qualified to operate from the carrier. Thereafter, regular exercises on board the ships ensured that the Harrier GR 7 force maintained a combat-ready capability for CVS operations.

In comparison to its predecessor, the Harrier GR 7 was much more suited to CVS operations – its larger wing and more powerful engine gave the aircraft better performance than the Harrier GR 3. 'Take-off was almost a non-event', explained Wg Cdr A D Stevenson, 'because the aircraft was launched into a parabolic curve [thanks to the carrier's ski-jump ramp], and since there was no drag, it accelerated quickly. The big wing of the GR 7 also created lift much more quickly than the GR 3 had done'.

The first step in planning a sortie from the deck was to calculate the exact distance needed for the aircraft to take off in its loaded configuration in the

An AIM-9L Sidewinder-armed Harrier GR 7 prepares for take-off from *Invincible* at the start of an NFZ sortie over southern Iraq during Operation *Bolton*. The ventral strakes that replaced the dummy gun pods are clearly visible from this aspect. The RAF Harrier GR 7 force began embarked operations in the mid-1990s, with the first operational deployment to the Persian Gulf for Operation *Bolton* occurring in January 1998 (*Crown Copyright/MoD*)

A pilot's eye view from the cockpit of a Harrier GR 7 while preparing to take off from *Ark Royal*. This image was taken during carrier operations in 2010 (*Crown Copyright/MoD*)

wind and temperature conditions of the day. If the aircraft hit the ramp too fast it would lose energy and slow down, but if it was too slow, the Harrier would not have sufficient speed to get airborne. Typically, the Harrier GR 7 needed a take-off run of between 450–600 ft. With ten degrees of nozzle set, the pilot slammed the throttle to full power before releasing the brakes and selecting 50 per cent nozzle as the aircraft became airborne. The major challenge during take-off was in judging the pitch of the deck to make sure that the brakes were not released until the pilot was sure that the aircraft would hit the ramp when the bow of the ship was above the horizon.

If take-off was considered to be relatively straightforward, landing was an altogether trickier manoeuvre. The first challenge was to find the ship, which had invariably moved some distance since take-off. With no airborne radar to help them, Harrier GR 7 pilots relied on navigating to the expected position of the ship and then finding it visually, or following the Tactical Air Navigation (TACAN) beacon on board the ship, or requesting that the ship's own radar help them recover to the carrier. Pilots were permitted to commit to the carrier once they had achieved two out of the three methods of visual, TACAN or radar contact.

Having located the ship, the Harrier had to be at its hovering weight before it could land. In order to achieve this relatively light weight, any fuel that would have enabled the aircraft to divert to a shore station had to be burnt off or dumped – in other words, the pilot was totally committed to landing on the ship. Thus, it was the landing weight of the aeroplane that determined what configuration of weapons could be carried at the start of the sortie. If, for example, the aircraft was loaded with two 1000-lb bombs, the fuel at hover weight would have to be 2000 lb less than that for an unloaded aeroplane (if the bombs were not dropped or jettisoned).

After arriving overhead the carrier at 2000 ft, the pilot flew a landing pattern that involved a descending orbit in order to arrive alongside the port side of the carrier in the hover at 90 ft above the sea. Although 'in the hover', the aircraft was actually matching the forward speed of the ship, which was typically about 20 knots. Next came a sideways transition to bring the aircraft over the deck at a height of 60 ft (the deck was approximately 30 ft above the waterline) to hover over the 'tram lines' painted on the flightdeck. The pilot then followed the signals of the deck marshaller to lower the aircraft on to the deck, often into a tight parking spot.

Not only did this whole manoeuvre require considerable skill, it was also to be carried out with no alternative option, since there was insufficient fuel to go anywhere else. There was also some time pressure, not only because of the rapidly depleting fuel but also because there was only approximately 90 seconds' worth of water injection which was needed by the engine to provide enough power for the hover. There was even more psychological pressure when there were other Harrier GR 7 pilots in the formation whose aircraft were also on minimum fuel, awaiting their turn to land.

If the landing manoeuvre was challenging during daylight, it was even more so at night, when the aircraft had to enter the hover with no outside visual cues. Flying on NVGs, pilots had a narrow field of vision, which meant they could either look forwards at the instruments in the HUD or turn their head through 90 degrees to look over their right shoulder at the ship. Balancing the scan between HUD and ship, with no other visual cues and no peripheral vision, was challenging even for the most experienced pilots.

On the night of 25 November 1997, Wg Cdr M A Leaky, OC No 1 Sqn, was lucky to survive when he hit the water during his approach to *Invincible* about 60 miles off Cagliari, Sardinia. During the final stages of his approach, the aircraft had begun to descend, but even the application of full power was insufficient to arrest the descent before the aircraft struck the water. The force of the impact rolled the aircraft onto its back and the pilot ejected downwards into the sea, but was fortunately rescued by a Sea King helicopter that was airborne in the vicinity. One of the safety recommendations made by the Board of Inquiry into the accident was that a more powerful variant of the Pegasus engine should be fitted to the Harrier GR 7, but it would be another six years before the Harrier GR 7A entered service.

OPERATION *BOLTON*

The night sortie flown by Wg Cdr Leaky was part of a work-up for deployment on Operation *Bolton* in the Middle East. In early November 1997, the Iraqis had declared that they would no longer cooperate with the UN Special COMmission (UNSCOM) inspectors that had been monitoring the nation's compliance with UN directives on biological and chemical warfare since the end of the Gulf War. As a result, the American-led Coalition reacted by increasing its military presence in the area, and *Invincible* was diverted from the Mediterranean Sea to the Persian Gulf, carrying eight Sea Harrier FA 2s and eight Harrier

GR 7s of No 1 Sqn. The ship had initially remained in the Mediterranean Sea as diplomatic moves and countermoves over Iraq ran their course in the UN over the winter months. During this time the Harriers flew missions over the Balkans in early December and again in early January 1998.

As the crisis deepened, *Invincible* sailed through the Suez Canal and arrived in the Persian Gulf in late January. Its aircraft started to fly patrols over Southern Iraq as part of Operation *Southern Watch* – the enforcement of the NFZ south of the 33rd Parallel – from 29 January. On each mission over Iraq, four LGB-armed Harrier GR 7s equipped with TIALD pods were escorted by four Sea Harriers.

However, in the end, neither the Tornado GR 1s based at Ali Al Salem air base in Kuwait nor the Harrier GR 7s on board *Invincible* were required to carry out attacks on targets in Iraq. Diplomatic initiatives had defused the crisis without the need for military intervention, and a new agreement between Iraq and UNSCOM was signed on 17 February. Nevertheless, the Harriers retained a presence in the region and continued to fly sorties in the Southern NFZ over Iraq for the next three months. The aircraft of No 1 Sqn were replaced in-theatre by those of No 3 Sqn during the first week of March when *Illustrious* relieved *Invincible*. *Illustrious* remained in the Persian Gulf for a month, leaving the region in mid-April.

A Harrier GR 7 of No 1 Sqn is towed through the hangar deck onto the lift prior to being brought up to the flightdeck of *Invincible* during Operation *Bolton*. A Sea Harrier FA 2 of 800 NAS is already lashed to the flightdeck (*Mark Zanker*)

JOINT FORCE HARRIER

In the Strategic Defence Review published in July 1998, the government elected in May of the previous year set out its future defence policy. This included the statement that 'the focus for our maritime forces in the new environment will move towards rapid deployment operations. Our amphibious capability with its improved specialised shipping will give our Rapid Reaction Forces important extra flexibility. Aircraft carriers will have a wide utility, including for deterrence and coercion. Our current Invincible class carriers will be given a wider power projection role by the development of a "Joint Force 2000" combining Royal Navy and RAF Harrier aircraft. To meet our longer-term needs, we plan to replace our current carriers from around 2012 with two larger, more versatile, carriers capable of carrying a more powerful force, including a future carrier borne aircraft to replace the Harrier'.

The Joint Force 2000 concept became the JFH reality on 1 April 2000, with the amalgamation of the Royal Navy Sea Harrier FA 2 and RAF Harrier GR 7 squadrons into a single unified command structure. Perhaps inevitably there were teething troubles with the new organisation, not least because of (sometimes petty) inter-service rivalry amongst some personnel, but on the whole the JFH concept worked well.

The first deployment of JFH was to participate in Exercise Linked Seas, which was to take place in the Atlantic Ocean off Portugal. Six Harrier GR 7s from No 3 Sqn, led by Wg Cdr Stevenson (OC No 3 Sqn), flew to Cagliari on 17 April 2000. The following day, the aircraft launched to embark on *Illustrious*, which had been exercising in the Mediterranean Sea with its compliment of Sea Harriers. On board the ship was a television crew with the presenter Alain de Cadenet, who was filming for the short-lived BBC series *Airshow*. For the Harrier pilots, that meant their first ever carrier landings would be under the spotlight of television cameras. The first to land was Wg Cdr Stevenson, who commented to de Cadenet afterwards that 'it was actually quite a psychological build up, as well as the physical training that had to be done, so I will admit to a certain trepidation!'

After arriving safely aboard *Illustrious*, the next task for the Harrier GR 7 pilots was to complete the five-sortie 'CVS work-up' syllabus before they could be considered fully qualified for CVS operations. This was achieved in the Mediterranean Sea over the next eight days. Although the emphasis was on taking off from and landing on the carrier, the pilots took advantage of the opportunity to practise

OPPOSITE
USS *George Washington* (CVN-73) sails past *Invincible* in the Persian Gulf in early 1998 during Operation *Bolton*. Both of the Harrier GR 7s in the foreground are carrying AIM-9L Sidewinder acquisition (training) rounds. Apart from the operational flying, the deployment also gave pilots the opportunity for some useful Dissimilar Air Combat Training (*Mark Zanker*)

Invincible at anchor off Bahrain during Operation *Bolton* in early 1998. The eight Harrier GR 7s of No 1 Sqn are identifiable by their slightly darker grey finish to that of the Sea Harrier FA 2s. *Invincible* remained in the Persian Gulf from January to March, when it was relieved by *Illustrious* and the Harrier GR 7s of No 3 Sqn and Sea Harriers of 801 NAS (*Crown Copyright/MoD*)

An AIM-9L-armed and TIALD-equipped Harrier GR 7 of No 3 Sqn lands aboard *Illustrious* in the Persian Gulf after a sortie during Operation *Bolton* on 12 March 1998 (*US National Archive*)

Air Combat Training (ACT) amongst themselves and with the Sea Harriers. With the work-up complete, the carrier sailed into position off the Portuguese coast on 27 April, ready for the start of the exercise. Unfortunately, however, poor weather in the shape of fog and low cloud across the region prevented any flying for the next few days.

Then came the order for *Illustrious* to head to Sierra Leone to support British operations there. The ship sailed at its best speed to reach the operational theatre as quickly as possible, but while maintaining this speed it was unable to launch and recover aircraft. So, as they travelled southwards, the Harrier pilots had to endure another four days of no flying.

Sierra Leone had been in the grip of a civil war since 1991. Over the years, various attempts by outside agencies to intervene and stop hostilities had failed, but in 1999 the Lomé Peace Accord appeared to be successful. It was followed by the deployment of the UN Assistance Mission in Sierra Leone to the country, but once again the agreements collapsed. When some 500 UN personnel were taken hostage by the Revolutionary United Front, the British government decided to settle things once and for all.

In Operation *Palliser*, British forces were despatched to secure the capital Freetown to evacuate British and other entitled personnel from the country. Troops from the Rapid Reaction Force were flown into Dakar, in neighbouring Senegal, by RAF Hercules, which also evacuated 500 civilians back to Britain. Meanwhile, *Illustrious* had arrived off West Africa on 3 May but was kept well out to sea 'beyond the horizon' so that its presence would be undetected. At first, the carrier's captain did not want to fly any aircraft in order to ensure that the ship was hidden from sight, but he was eventually persuaded that the pilots needed to remain in currency and a flying programme started on 4 May. Over the next 12 days, the Harriers flew sorties close to the ship, comprising ACT and also bombing a splash target towed by the vessel, practising 20- and 30-degree dive-bombing profiles.

Wg Cdr Stevenson led the first operational sortie by the new JFH on 17 May. His formation consisted of two Harrier GR 7s (flown by himself and Sqn Ldr R McCormack), each armed with two 540-lb bombs, accompanied by two Sea Harriers. The mission was to carry out a Show Of Presence over the population centres of Sierra Leone and the airport at Lungi, some ten miles to the north of, and across the bay from, Freetown. In order for this to make sufficient impact, the sortie had to be carried out at very low-level, but that exposed the aircraft to three threats. Firstly, there was the possibility of running into small arms fire from the rebels; secondly, there was a real risk of a bird strike with the huge raptors that nested in the jungle canopy; and thirdly, the risk of hitting one of the occasional extra-tall tree trunks that extended well above the main canopy, but were virtually invisible against the background of trees.

Since several of the 'old hands' had lots of experience of flying over similar terrain in Belize, jungle flying did not present a major challenge. However, Stevenson was taken aback by the lack of any planning for SAR in the event of a pilot having to eject over the jungle. As it turned out, the greatest challenge during the sortie was the recovery to the ship, Stevenson later explaining 'there were two levels of fear – firstly in finding the carrier without a radar, and secondly landing on it with ever diminishing fuel'.

In order to achieve a hover weight that would enable them to land in the tropical heat, and with the 1100-lb weight of the two bombs still loaded, the pilots had to burn down well below their diversion fuel to around 1500 lbs. Since the minimum landing fuel was 800 lbs and the landing manoeuvre burnt 500–600 lbs, there was little margin for error.

Another Show Of Presence was flown on 19 May, and the results of the two missions were so successful that further such flights were not deemed necessary for the next two weeks. Instead, the Harrier GR 7 pilots started a night work-up so that they could operate from the ship in darkness in case they were tasked to fly any night missions. They also flew some ACT sorties and, on both 29 May and 1 June, carried out CAS training with a land-based FAC in Sierra Leone. In another development, the Harrier GR 7s were involved in contingency planning to support SF in the event of a hostage rescue mission.

It is perhaps surprising that the aircraft were retained on board the ship during Operation *Palliser* when the airport at Lungi might have been an ideal 'austere operating strip' for Harrier operations. Pilots certainly found it frustrating that, having deployed to Sierra Leone, there seemed to be little political will or operational tasking to use their capabilities. After flying a last low-level Show of Presence over Freetown and Lungi on 5 June, *Illustrious* headed home. The Harrier GR 7s launched from the carrier six days later as the ship sailed abeam Lisbon, with No 3 Sqn flying directly to Wittering.

A Harrier GR 7 pilot of No 3 Sqn carries out cockpit checks on the flightdeck of *Illustrious* prior to launching for an Operation *Bolton* mission on 12 March 1998 (*US National Archive*)

CHAPTER FOUR

KOSOVO

Sqn Ldr 'Benny' Ball, the Executive Officer of No 1 Sqn, taxies out for a mission over Kosovo. Sqn Ldr Ball was awarded a Distinguished Flying Cross for his gallantry during Operation *Engadine*. Note the bomb symbols painted in black below the cockpit, each representing a sortie when weapons were expended (*Martin Ball*)

Air operations over Bosnia-Herzegovina, which had continued in support of the NATO Stabilisation Force, were scaled back in June 1998 and became Operation *Deliberate Forge*. But just as peace was being established in Bosnia, tensions in neighbouring Kosovo exploded into violence, and by the autumn, another full-scale war had erupted in the region. After a brief respite from the Balkans, four Harrier GR 7s replaced the four Jaguars at Gioia del Colle in July 1998, taking on the responsibility for operations over Bosnia.

Meanwhile, attempts were made to resolve the conflict through diplomacy, but as the situation deteriorated further, four more Harriers deployed to Gioia del Colle on 20 January 1999. The RAF contribution to the NATO forces involved in operations over the Former Republic of Yugoslavia now comprised eight Harrier GR 7s from No 3 Sqn, supported by two TriStar tankers operating from Ancona. In February, No 1 Sqn arrived at Gioia del Colle to relieve No 3 Sqn.

'Strangely we arrived by Alitalia and got a hire car to Gioia del Colle', Sqn Ldr M G Ball recalled. 'The last time I had left Gioia del Colle, just over a year earlier, I had been told not to return ever again after accidentally bombing a nearby farmyard. An elderly couple were sitting on the terrace of their farmhouse watching the sunset when they saw two 1000-lb bombs detach from my Harrier GR 7 whilst on the approach to the airfield. The bombs bounced, ricocheted off a farm wall and came to rest on either side of the farmhouse. The bombs remained intact, as they had accidentally been jettisoned, and I kept my job due to an anomaly in the system. This didn't stop the boys from ribbing me, and threatening to tell the guards that I was back. So started our deployment. Having just completed an operation on the aircraft carrier as well as a Red Flag exercise and a heavy weapons detachment in the USA, we felt as ready as we could be'.

After a massacre of Kosovan Albanians at Račak in mid-January, NATO members agreed to take collective military action, if needed, to enforce a solution. First, however, a conference was held at Rambouillet, in France, in February, at which the NATO Secretary General, Javier Solana, attempted to facilitate a political settlement between the two sides in Kosovo. Unfortunately, the negotiations led nowhere, and on 24 March NATO decided that the only option was to resort to military force. This was known as Operation *Allied Force*, of which the British component was codenamed Operation *Engadine*.

Sqn Ldr Ball remembered that 'the afternoon before the first night mission, we were in another pre-op brief when the boss got called out by one of the Intelligence Officers. "Boss, the Prime Minister is on the phone for you". We now knew it was on. As Exec on the squadron, I am involved in picking the team for night one, but also as Exec I know that it won't include me! We lead from the front, and so it is the Boss who will lead the first formation into battle. My reward will be to lead Night Two.

'The first night is surreal, as I witness the team prepare and plan for an event they have been training for since their flying careers began. As the pilots prepare to out-brief, word comes through that there is a problem with the software programming of the RWR. Apparently, an F-16 radar lock appears as an enemy SAM system, and some F-16s have been planned into the strike just ahead of the squadron formation. It is now too late to re-plan, and the only strategy that can be adopted is to treat the threat as a real SAM and evade if necessary. Bizarrely, as the formation prepare to leave the ops room, the Red Arrows pilots, who are en route to their winter training destination, appear in the ops room. Whilst the Red Arrows pilots are made to feel welcome by fellow colleagues on our squadron, they soon realise that they are the bridesmaids tonight and not the bride and make themselves scarce!'

Wg Cdr A Golledge (OC No 1 Sqn) led six Harriers on the first offensive mission of Operation *Engadine* over Kosovo on the night of 24 March. The formation comprised two pairs of self-designating bombers, loaded with LGBs, with another 'spotter' aircraft in each section whose task it was to watch out for SAM launches while the bombers were 'heads in' designating their targets.

'The bus ride through the darkness out to the aircraft was a quiet one, with a definite lack of the usual banter being exchanged between pilots', recalled Flt Lt M W Zanker, who would be flying as No 2 to Wg Cdr Golledge. 'The weather was kind to us that night and we managed to RV [rendezvous] successfully with the VC10K tanker. Tanking was done lights out using NVGs and in radio silence, and I distinctly remember thinking that the other formations looked dangerously close when viewed through the goggles as they took fuel from their respective tankers in adjacent areas.

'On the way to the target we heard a Dutch F-16 ahead of us request

During Operation *Engadine*, the Harriers were supported by a TriStar tanker from No 216 Sqn. The TriStar had just a single refuelling hose, so only one aircraft could be refuelled at a time. Here, a Harrier refuels while the other looks on (*Mark Zanker*)

permission to engage a fast-moving contact coming south from Belgrade. The AWACS controller made him wait for what seemed like an age, and the Dutchman was getting more and more agitated, concerned that his target would elude him. He finally received permission to fire.'

The Harrier pilots had heard Maj Peter Tankink of No 322 Sqn Royal Netherlands Air Force detect and then shoot down a Serbian MiG-29 with an AIM-120 missile. Zanker continued;

'As well as fighter cover ahead of us, there were also a number of SEAD assets who would fly in above us and launch anti-radiation missiles into the target area. These things looked spectacular when viewed through NVGs. The rocket motor burned brightly as the missile accelerated out in front of the launch aircraft, then it would pitch up into a steep climb. The motor would burn out soon after, but you could still see the glow through the NVGs as it arced out ahead. We never saw them land, but the Serbs soon got the idea that it was foolish to turn on any threat radars because these things were deadly.

'There was also quite a bit of communications jamming on some of the strike frequencies. The Serbs would play music or recordings of previous radio transmissions. The latter were quite distracting, but nothing that we couldn't cope with.

'As we ran in towards the target area, we began to see bomb flashes from other elements of the package ahead. There was some broken cloud cover too, and together with the drifting smoke from the detonating bombs, it became more and more difficult to positively identify our targets. The message from the Prime Minister before we left was loud and clear – if in doubt, do not drop, and so we all returned from the first mission without releasing a single weapon. It was a disappointing start to the campaign, but we all knew it had been the right decision.'

The following night, a second mission by six Harriers led by Sqn Ldr Ball successfully targeted a military complex at Leskovac, but the eight aircraft that launched on 26 March for the Pristina explosive storage facility were recalled because heavy clouds over Kosovo obscured the target area.

The weather also prevented Harrier operations the next night. This experience was typical of the Kosovo campaign – poor weather conditions over the Balkans made it difficult to employ LGBs, which need a clear line of sight between designator and target throughout an attack.

On 27 March, four more Harriers arrived at Gioia del Colle, bringing the detachment strength to 12 aircraft, and a further two TriStars and three VC10Ks deployed to Ancona to bolster the AAR detachment.

The following day, *The Sunday Times* published a story under the headline 'RAF Officials Admit to Frustration Over Harrier Missions' in which it alleged that 'Senior RAF officers have admitted to frustration at the level of unsuccessful Harrier GR 7 bombing missions over Serbia, but deny that the aircraft's performance has become an embarrassment. During the first three nights of bombing, 20 Harrier flights were launched, but only two scored direct hits on Serbian targets. Poor visibility and "technical problems" have been given as explanations'. The journalists responsible for the article had failed to consider the strict rules of engagement in place over Serbia, and the hostile publicity generated by their story was not helpful to the Harrier detachment.

That night (28 March), as he planned an attack on a munitions depot in Pristina, Sqn Ldr Ball felt that 'the pressure was on to deliver, and we had to ensure that tonight's mission was a success as we now had a new enemy – the press. The first pilots I called into the plan were the two QWIs. This mission was all about hitting the targets successfully, and I wanted to give the QWIs all the time they needed. Their job was to decide on the best direction for the attack and select the best fuse settings for the 1000-lb LGB weapons.

'With the QWIs, I had to decide whether to conduct self-designated attacks or to buddy spike the targets. There are many arguments in favour of both self-designation and buddy spiking, but on that night, with the added pressures to succeed, we opted for buddy spiking attacks. Of note also was the fact that the target tonight was much further into enemy territory, increasing the risk of exposure to enemy attacks mainly from the ground but possibly from the air as well. It took us a good four hours to come up with the target plan. At least tonight we were not flying in behind the F-16s!

'This was the first real op for all of us that would be opposed by an angry enemy. It made the planning complicated. A simple in and out mission with one set of targets was intensified by the "what if" considerations such as threats, evasion, timing slips and loser plans. It was easy to get information overload and forget that this was all about attacking one target.

'It was almost a relief to finally get to the aircraft that was fully prepped and sitting in the HAS [hardened aircraft shelter]. You could feel the tension in the air as you climbed the ladder and settled down in the tight-fitting cockpit, alone at last with only your thoughts and the task ahead. I loaded my planning brick and checked the route – everything was there, every waypoint, all the timings. Every aspect of a mission is timed, from the Have Quick check-in to the engine start-up, taxi, take-off, the airborne hold and, of course, the arrival time at the target.

'Success of the Have Quick secure radio check-in had been limited in training, but now that we were using it all the time, it worked perfectly.

Taxiing out at Gioia del Colle for a mission over Kosovo, Harrier GR 7 ZD329 is loaded with 1000-lb Paveway II LGBs. Unlike in Operation *Vulcan*, during which the Harriers had to use TIALD-equipped Jaguars to mark targets for cooperative attacks, the Harriers participating in Operation *Engadine* were able to carry the TIALD pod themselves and self-designate targets (*Crown Copyright/MoD*)

For the early part of this mission, everything was running smoothly, apart from feeling hot and steaming up. Whilst taxiing out to the runway I opened the canopy to let some air in, and I soon decided that the protective laser glasses had to go! It was too dark with them on, especially as we were also wearing NVGs. I'd have to take the risk of suffering laser damage to my eyes.

'Soon, we were all airborne, including the spare aircraft. We were quickly feet wet, checking our chaff system, MAW and missiles and talking to Mission Control, as well as listening out for any slips to the timings. Whilst in the hold I selected the target waypoint, which was more than 200 nautical miles away. It was going to be a long time in the combat area. The first mission of the night, being flown by USAF F-117 stealth fighters, was on its way out, and now it was our turn.

'On time and with no mission delay, we headed off on our routing and over the border. It was eerily quiet, and we were the lead tonight, so there would be no smoke obscuring our target. The RWR also remained quiet, and we were now approaching the IP [Initial Point] – everything was going so quickly.

'It was time to start searching for the target using my TIALD pod. I was the spiker and my No 2 was the bomber. The system for finding the target was to go from zoomed out scale, big picture, to zoomed in. This was not as easy in the cockpit as it was when using the computer simulator in the ops room. Time was running out as we approached the target.

'Zoom out and acquire the target area, then zoom in and acquire the target. Zoom in too much and there would be excessive pixilation on the small black and white screen I was looking at. It was time to call "target acquired" to my No 2 – was that the target? Yes, it was. Track the target, fire the laser and listen for the tone of the bombs coming off. Nothing! No 2 hang up! What? Bomb hang-up! This wasn't the plan! We started our escape from the target area – two right hand turns reversing our route, placing us 15 nautical miles away from the target.

'We could now only hope that the second and third pair had better luck. They were a minute behind – time for us to escape and look back into the area. We heard the tone of the weapons release and waited for half-a-minute as the 1000-lb bombs sought out the laser and flew to the target. There was an almighty flash, followed by a second flash a minute later – success! Wary of the fact that we were still in enemy territory, we climbed and then headed home.

'On landing, we were met by the groundcrew with handshakes and beers. The war stories then started as we signed the F700s, after which it was off to the ops room to look at the tapes of the attacks and debrief. There were many lessons to be learned of course, with the bomb hang-up being traced to a pylon release issue. My target acquisition with the TIALD pod needed some more polish, but above all we had delivered two sets of weapons on to the correct targets. The results were sent to the MoD and we had our first success story for the press!'

Numerous sorties were aborted over the next week when they encountered poor weather over the Balkans. Although these missions did not reach their targets, they were nevertheless flying over hostile territory, with the attendant risks. During a mission led by Wg Cdr Golledge against Urosevac barracks on 30 March, the six-ship formation was forced to turn back east of Skopje. Flt Lt Zanker, flying as No 5 in the formation, noted 'heavy calibre AAA observed close to the Kosovo–Macedonia border, SA-6 launches reported near Pristina and Urosevac'.

Despite the limitations imposed by the weather, the Serbian air defence network had been sufficiently degraded for daylight operations to commence on 4 April. Until now, the Harriers had been loaded with AIM-9Ls for self-defence, but with the Serbian Air Force no longer a threat, the missiles became an incumbrance because of the arming and dis-arming procedures associated with forward-firing weapons. It was therefore decided that it was no longer necessary to carry the Sidewinders. However, the threat from AAA and man-portable infrared (IR) SAMs over Kosovo and Serbia had not diminished.

Daylight CAS missions involved flying in pairs to pre-arranged holding points over Albania or Macedonia. Here, armed with upgraded RBL755 or 1000-lb freefall bombs, the Harrier pair would orbit whilst awaiting tasking from a USAF Airborne FAC (AFAC) in an A-10 or F-16. The AFAC would then direct the Harriers to a suitable target. If there was no such target, each mission was also given a 'dump target', such as a barracks or storage facility, that would be attacked in lieu of a 'traditional' battlefield CAS target. Unfortunately, despite launching CAS missions each day, the Harriers were unable to push into Kosovo itself for the first two days of CAS tasking because of low cloud cover.

The weather improved on 6 April, allowing ten Harriers to carry out daylight CAS sorties against four groups of Serbian ground forces in Kosovo. In the case of Flt Lts Zanker and C J Averty, the target was a vehicle assembly area near Prizren. For Sqn Ldr Atha and Flt Lt P N Mounsey, it was a convoy to the east of Peć that was marked by an A-10 AFAC, and on which they dropped four RBL755s. That night, another wave of Harriers bombed an ammunition facility in Kosovo, while six Tornados operating from Brüggen attacked Pristina barracks. The next day (7 April) brought mixed fortunes for the ten Harriers led by Flt Lt M M E V Garland. Neither Flt Lt Zanker with Capt Cockerell, nor Sqn Ldr Ball with Flt Lt Averty, were given targets, but Sqn Ldr Atha and Flt Lt Mounsey dropped four RBL755s on a vehicle compound, again under the direction of an A-10 AFAC.

After losing another day dogged by poor weather, Harrier operations resumed on 8 April with ten sorties, led by Sqn Ldr Ball, mounted into

A pair of Harrier GR 7s loaded with 1000-lb freefall bombs and each equipped with a DJRP bank over clouds above the Balkans. Low cloud frequently prevented LGB operations during Operation *Engadine*, and around one-third of LGB attacks had to be aborted because of the weather conditions. However, the GPS-fed weapon aiming system in the Harrier GR 7 enabled pilots to strike their targets with remarkable accuracy using freefall bombs even when they were obscured by cloud (*Crown Copyright/MoD*)

Kosovo. Ball and Flt Lt Averty were tasked by an A-10 AFAC against vehicles close to four barns to the southwest of Dakovica (Gjakova), which they attacked with RBL755s. Meanwhile, there were no targets for Flt Lts Zanker and Mounsey, who were instead sent to a TriStar tanker to refuel. Despite flying a two-and-a-half-hour sortie, they were not used by the AFAC.

There was still a lack of CAS targets two days later, so the six Harriers that launched for a daylight CAS mission were directed to attack a military storage area at Pristina and a radio relay station. Moreover, eight sorties tasked that night against military vehicles were recalled because the targets had moved location.

On 11 April Sqn Ldr Ball led another ten-ship CAS mission, with Flt Lt D Killeen acting as his No 2. In a sortie that lasted nearly four hours, the Harriers refuelled twice, firstly from a Boeing 707 and then from a TriStar, before being tasked by an F-16 AFAC onto a convoy near Malisevo. Extensive cloud cover made it difficult to see the target, and at one point an SA-6 launch was called, but there was no sign of a missile. Eventually, Ball was able to locate the target using binoculars, and he identified it as being made up of civilian vehicles.

Meanwhile, Flt Lts Zanker and Averty, with Sqn Ldr Atha and Flt Lt Mounsey, were scrambled from ground alert (known as Ground CAS (GCAS)), each with two 1000-lb bombs, which they dropped through cloud using the 'GPS Auto' function in the weapon aiming system on to the position of a suspected SA-6 site. The next day, after a lengthy ground hold, Flt Lt Zanker led ten Harriers to Kosovo for a CAS mission. However, the weather was not good in the area and the aircraft were directed to their dump targets, which were a Petrol Oil and Lubricant (POL) depot, a military radio relay station and a military radar in Kosovo. Again, the bombs were dropped through cloud using GPS, and the accuracy of the attack was confirmed when Sqn Ldr Ball filmed the target with his TIALD pod and was able to report that the oil storage depot was seen to be burning.

It was a similar story on 13 April when Sqn Ldr Ball led Flt Lts Averty and Zanker and Capt Cockerell – each of their aircraft armed with 1000-lb freefall bombs – on a CAS mission in southern Serbia. With thick cloud in the area, they were re-tasked against a POL depot at Pristina. During the transit to this target, an SA-6 was launched against the formation, and Ball was forced to defend against it using manoeuvre and chaff. The pilots made successful attacks, but were also fired on by AAA as they egressed. Meanwhile, since there were no CAS targets, Sqn Ldr Atha and Flt Lt Mounsey each dropped four RBL755s through cloud on to the radar site Kosovska Mitrovica.

Locating battlefield targets was challenging, especially when they were hidden, but the Harrier pilots came up with an ingenious solution, as Flt Lt Zanker described;

'For a time we did fit the LOROP recce pod on the centreline pylon and ran the vertical camera whenever we were over Kosovo during our tasked missions. The RIC at Gioia discovered a lot of hidden Serb equipment in barns and woodland and they passed the coordinates to the A-10 squadron that was also at Gioia. This was quite successful until [the air operations centre at] Aviano found out about our in-house targeting arrangement and stopped it.'

Wg Cdr Golledge led six Harriers on a CAS mission on 14 April, and once again the aircraft were re-tasked to their dump target – an ammunition depot at Pristina. Because of the weather, the bombs were dropped through the cloud using 'GPS Auto' delivery, but once again Sqn Ldr Ball was able to confirm the accuracy of the attack. He recalled, 'the weather cleared and I successfully filmed my bombs severely damaging the building with the TIALD pod'.

Meanwhile, two more pairs, one led by Capt Cockerell and the other by Flt Lt Zanker, had been tasked by an F-16 AFAC to attack a large vehicle convoy near Dakovica. 'That certainly seemed strange to me because the Serbs were not in the habit of parking military vehicles on a road in broad daylight', commented Zanker. 'I could see a straight road that came from the town for a mile or so before crossing a large river. Between the town and the river was a long column of vehicles parked by the side of the road. Through the binoculars, I could just make out a few Armoured Personnel Carriers (APCs) at each end of the convoy, but most of the vehicles were tractors connected to trailers. Some of the tractors were red and the fields adjacent to the road were full of people. We four Harrier pilots discussed the target on our own in-house frequency and quickly concluded that this was a convoy of refugees that were being herded by Serb soldiers'.

The Harrier pilots persuaded an A-10 to take a closer look, and it was then confirmed that the convoy was indeed a civilian one. When they returned to Gioia del Colle, the pilots discovered that another civilian convoy in the same area had been bombed by F-16s earlier in the day, causing considerable embarrassment to NATO.

There were no CAS targets for the ten Harriers led by Sqn Ldr Ball into the operational area the following day (15 April), so they were split between two static targets. Six were tasked with bombing the barracks to the west of Pristina that was used by the Serbian paramilitary commander Željko Ražnatović, better known as 'Arkan'. Ball and Flt Lt Averty claimed successful delivery of their RBL755s against the target, but Flt Lt Zanker saw his own weapons fall into woods 500 m short of the buildings. This problem was not unknown, as A-10 AFAC Capt N S Brauner observed;

'The Harriers were normally great to work with because they had actually been trained for CAS, which meant they were proficient at looking outside the cockpit to visually acquire targets. Even though we weren't flying CAS missions in Kosovo, what we were doing required many of the same strengths and skills. We saw a big difference between pilots who trained to acquire targets visually and those who trained to bomb coordinates.

It was much easier to talk the first group on to targets. The Harrier pilots could be expected to find the target visually, but their [RBL]755s hit short almost every time because of a software glitch in their aiming and delivery system.'

Meanwhile, the remaining four Harriers had bombed armoured vehicles in revetments in eastern Kosovo. The 'Arkan' barracks was also successfully attacked the following day by four Harriers led by Flt Lt Garland.

Flt Lt Zanker led the first daytime TIALD/Paveway II attack on 19 April. The target was an SA-6 and fuel storage depot near Pristina airport that had previously appeared on the target list for a mission on 29 March, although on that occasion the attack had been foiled by the weather. This time conditions were better, and the plan was for attacks by two pairs of Harriers. In each case the element leader would carry out a self-designated drop of two LGBs while the wingman watched out for SAM launches, before dropping his own 1000-lb freefall bombs on the compound.

'As we ran in, there was some cumulus cloud at around 10,000 ft, but I reckoned the area would be clear enough to hit the target', recalled Zanker. 'I brought the

Armourers from No 1 Sqn complete the loading of a 1000-lb Paveway II LGB to the underwing pylon of a Harrier GR 7 at Gioia del Colle. The aircraft is armed with an AIM-9L Sidewinder. Note, too, the BOL chaff dispensers which are integral to the front of the missile rail. They enabled the Harrier to carry self-protective chaff without losing a weapons pylon. Another BOL rail is also visible in the foreground, on the outermost underwing pylon (*Crown Copyright/MoD*)

TIALD seeker out of its parked position and it immediately slewed to the target location. I could see the compound and buildings on the cockpit screen. As it was not exactly on the planned target, I manually slewed the crosshairs with my left hand using the thumb ball on the throttle and then pressed down on the controller, commanding the seeker to track the target. Everything looked good for a drop, and so I pressed the other button on the throttle to fire the TIALD laser. With the weapon aiming set to drop the bombs automatically, I held the button down until the computer released them with a double clunk and I heard the high-pitched tone in the headset that indicated the bombs had gone.

'After about five seconds, a fluffy white cloud appeared in the top of the screen and moved down towards the crosshairs. At this point the TIALD should have gone into memory mode to keep it roughly pointing at the target, but it didn't. Instead, it decided to track the ever-changing edge of the fluffy white cloud and off it went. With a mind of its own, the seeker shot off somewhere I didn't know, and it was clearly looking nowhere near the target that the two bombs were now dropping towards. I parked the seeker head and then un-parked it, which I hoped would get it to lock back on to the target. With only a few seconds left I managed to rapidly re-acquire the building, get the crosshairs back on to the centre of the roof and fire the laser. Miraculously, the freefalling LGBs both managed to re-lock to the reflected laser light and had enough energy to steer themselves right into the centre of the building with a huge flash.'

Flt Lt Averty followed up with his freefall bombs, before the next pair led by Sqn Ldr Ball made their attack. About 15 miles to their south, the building for the HQ unit at Urosevac (Ferizaj) airfield was bombed by Sqn Ldr Atha and Flt Lt Mounsey.

A week of poor weather followed, during which most of the few sorties that were launched were unable to enter the operational area. However, Sqn Ldr Ball and Flt Lt Leach did drop four RBL755s through cloud on to a command centre at Podujevo on 22 April, and Sqn Ldr Atha with Flt Lt A J E Cullen dropped RBL755s on an artillery site to the east of Urosevac two days later. The weather had improved a little by 27 April, when Sqn Ldr P Kosogorin and Flt Lt Zanker took off in fog from Gioia del Colle for the former to drop a 2000-lb Paveway III bomb on a bridge to the north of Pristina. Zanker recorded that 'the weapon was released in ideal conditions and the target was lased, but the weapon was not seen to impact'. Later in the day, a total of 15 Harrier sorties were generated from Gioia del Colle to target an ammunition storage facility at Besinje, but the aircraft had to drop their bombs through cloud.

The 11 Harrier missions flown on 28 April included attacks by two pairs on a radio relay station on the hills south of Prizren, and an attack on Podgorica airfield in Montenegro by three aircraft led by Flt Lt J G Doidge. This latter mission was part of a larger NATO strike on the base, which included a formation of F-16s. Two aircraft, flown by Doidge and Sqn Ldr Ball, planned to carry out self-designated LGB attacks respectively on a hangar and a maintenance building. The airfield itself was defended by an SA-6, so the No 3 pilot, Flt Lt H Smyth, was employed as a 'spotter' to watch for any missile launches during the most vulnerable phase of the attack while Doidge and Ball were heads in the cockpit, concentrating on the laser tracking. According to Sqn Ldr Ball;

'The weather approaching the target area was not good! It wasn't long before I found myself in thick cloud, unsighted from "Doidgy" and "Harv". My Have Quick radios were also crackling loudly to the extent that I couldn't hear any calls – this may have been caused by either deliberate radio jamming or weather interference. I now felt like I was on my own, unable to tell whether the attack was still going ahead. With no other indications available to me, and still in cloud, I decided to start the attack on time, for at least as a formation we were height deconflicted. With a minute to run to the target, the skies started to clear, and, with relief, "Doidgy" and "Harv" appeared out of the wispy edges of the cloud. Now the skies had cleared, the targets were easy to acquire and were successfully attacked.'

Despite the challenges of the weather and the defences, the mission was successful, and both targets were destroyed. The next day, the detachment was reinforced with the addition of four more Harrier GR 7s.

Eighteen sorties were flown on 30 April, with Flt Lt Zanker leading three pairs to carry out cooperative LGB attacks against the bridge over the River Uvac at Kokin Brod, in western Serbia. Within each pair, the leader would mark the target for bombs dropped by the wingman.

Former Red Arrows pilot and QWI Ft Lt Mark Zanker was Mentioned in Dispatches for his work during Operation *Engadine*. Note the impressive tally of 25 bomb symbols beneath the cockpit, representing the operational missions flown by that particular aircraft (*Mark Zanker*)

As they ran in to the target area, the Harrier pilots found themselves sandwiched between a layer of stratus cloud above them and rising ground below.

'Getting close to the release point, I could also see that there was more cumulus cloud between us and the target', recalled Zanker. 'I looked up from my screen and scanned ahead to the target area. It looked clear. With only a few seconds to go to bomb release, I still couldn't see the target in the crosshairs but I was confident that there would be enough tracking time to get a hit. My No 2 released his bombs and after about five seconds the cloud cleared, and I saw the bridge. This time I dispensed with the auto-track function and zoomed in on the bridge. I could now see that it was a three-arch viaduct, and so I manually slewed the crosshairs to the centre of a span. The laser fired and every now and again I would nudge the crosshairs back to the target if they started to drift off. The bombs seemed to take an age to reach the bridge, but when they hit, the explosion was spectacular'.

The bombs from the second pair missed the target when smoke from the first detonations obscured the bridge, causing the laser to lose lock, but in the third pair, Sqn Ldr Ball guided the bombs to another hit close to the first. In the debrief back at Gioia del Colle, the pilots reviewed their TIALD videos on a television screen. Ball explained;

'On the big screen you could see so much more than you could on the four-inch screen in the aircraft. We watched the TIALD on lock slew to the target area, zoom in to find the six-span bridge, slew to an abutment and track. From the top of the screen a vehicle appeared, slowly heading towards the bridge. There was no way this could have been seen looking at the screen in the aircraft, but on the big screen we saw it immediately. "Oh no", we exclaimed, "How long has he got?" Slowly, the vehicle approached the bridge and then there was the tone of the bombs being released. "He has less than 40 seconds".

'The vehicle was now on the bridge and approaching the abutment that was being tracked, and the laser was firing, successfully flashing, awaiting the inevitable. The bombs were in the air and the car was slowly approaching the abutment. "Why is he going so slowly? Come on mate, put your foot down!" We were talking to the screen as though this was live, although his fate had already been sealed a couple of hours earlier. With 20 seconds to go, he drove right through the laser tracker. "Go, Go, Go" we shouted at the screen. Some guys came in to see what the commotion was. The car moved over the bridge still in the blast area and eventually started to climb up the hill on the other side as the screen went white with the blast of the two 1000-lb bombs. As the screen cleared, we could see that the car had stopped. There was silence as we waited, and then we saw the car drive off at speed! A lucky day for him and us!'

Twelve Harriers attacked an army barracks and rail bridge at Djakovica, in Serbia, on 1 May. That same day, Sqn Ldr Ball led a four-ship comprising himself and Flt Lt Killeen as designators for Flt Lt Mounsey (armed with a 2000-lb Paveway III bomb) and Flt Lt P Leach (armed with two 1000-lb Paveway II bombs) against the airfield at Sjenica, in southwestern Serbia. The front pair aborted the mission after suffering a failure with their ECM equipment and the rear pair could not drop because the target was obscured by cloud. Flt Lt Zanker and Capt Cockerell also experienced frustration when they tried, unsuccessfully, to locate a 'Flat Face' radar on the southern coastal tip of Montenegro.

Although more than 30 sorties were flown against Serbian army and police units in Kosovo over the next three days, poor weather prevented many of the aircraft involved from releasing their weapons. Wg Cdr Golledge later wrote that when his pilots 'were trusted to lead missions and attack targets, they did so with meticulous regard for the rules of engagement and to minimise the risks of any civilian death, injury or damage. Indeed, if ever the pilots were in any doubt about the targets, they did not drop their munitions'.

The weather continued to adversely affect Harrier missions for the first fortnight of May, but Sjenica airfield was attacked again on 7 May in an operation led by Sqn Ldr Atha, with 1000-lb bombs being dropped through cloud. Atha was in action again the next day, leading Flt Lt Averty on what he described as an 'awesome CAS sortie'. Controlled by an A-10 AFAC, the Harriers carried out two attacks on APCs and artillery with RBL755 and 1000-lb airburst bombs.

Conditions improved on 14 May when Sqn Ldr C J R Norton led Flt Lts Killeen, S Adey and Mounsey, Sqn Ldr Ball and Capt Cockerell in an attack on the barracks at Krusevac and a river bridge near Nis, some 30 miles to the southeast. The leader of each pair was to designate the barracks, prior to carrying out his own self-designated attack on the four-lane road over the river bridge.

Meanwhile, Sqn Ldr Atha led four Paveway II-loaded Harriers against the Grdelica rail bridge (five miles southeast of Lekovac). The element leaders 'spiked' for their wingmen, before self-designating their own weapons. The bombs dropped by Flt Lt Holmes hit the target seconds before clouds obscured the bridge, scoring what Atha described as 'a lucky hit'. Atha used the same tactics the next day for his four-ship attack against the Kosmaka road bridge, while four more Harriers targeted another bridge to the south. Once again, good hits were obtained. That same day, Sqn Ldr Ball and Flt Lt Holmes attacked a small convoy near Velika Krusa, but on a separate mission Flt Lts Zanker and C A Margiotta were unable to find any suitable targets.

The weather then intervened again, resulting in Harrier sorties being restricted.

Two RBL755 cluster bombs loaded under the wings of a Harrier GR 7 at Gioia del Colle. The RBL755 was fitted with a radar altimeter to enable it to be dropped from medium-level, whereas the earlier BL755 could only be delivered from low-level. A load like this was typical for many of the CAS missions flown by Harriers over Kosovo (*Mark Zanker*)

Blurred by the exhaust efflux from their Pegasus engines, a four-ship of Harrier GR 7s all armed with four RBL755 cluster bombs taxi out at Gioia del Colle for a CAS mission in support of Operation *Engadine*. Note the extended AAR probes (*Crown Copyright/MoD*)

On 17 May Sqn Ldr Atha had a busy time dealing with poor conditions when he led a four-ship against the Tomance bridge, having had to abort a mission against the same target the previous day. The initial attack was foiled by low clouds, but after taking Flt Lt D P Kane to a KC-10 tanker, the pair returned two hours later and made several more attempts. A final effort from the south that saw Atha designate the Paveway IIs dropped by Kane was successful. 'TIALD runs off after bomb release', wrote Atha. 'Frantic re-acquisition results in ten seconds of lasing. Two Direct Hits – target destroyed. Undoubtedly *the* sortie of *Allied Force* for me'.

After a brief break, Harrier operations continued on 21 May, including a sortie in which Flt Lt A McKeon, Sqn Ldr Ball and Flt Lt Margiotta were tasked by an F-16 AFAC against a military compound at Durakovac (Gjurakoc). Ball described how 'using the binoculars, our leader [McKeon] noticed that there were multi-coloured cars in a nearby car park – civilian cars. Something didn't compute, and on closer inspection we could see that there was barbed wire, watch towers and lighting bordering the compound. This was not a military compound – it was a civilian prison. Ahead of us were some Coalition F-16 fighter-bombers, and Flt Lt McKeon successfully called off the attack'.

Later that same day Wg Cdr Golledge led three Harriers against a Serbian border surveillance post known as the 'Cafe Marrizit'. The building was so small that it was identified too late to attack on the first pass, but on the second pass Flt Lt Earl, flying in the No 2 jet, scored a direct hit on the post.

Most of the 18 Harrier sorties on 22 May saw pilots unable to release their weapons because of the weather conditions (only two were successful), and 48 hours later, only eight sorties were flown out of a planned total of 20. However, the following day brought better weather, although Flt Lts Zanker and Earl had to drop their freefall bombs through cloud when they attacked a storage depot to the west of Pristina. On the other hand, Sqn Ldr Ball and Flt Lt Averty were able to drop four RBL755s on to revetments south of Vranje that had been marked by an F-16 AFAC using white phosphorous rockets.

Twenty sorties were flown over Kosovo by the Harrier GR 7s on 26 May. Over 29 and 30 May, Harriers attacked vehicles, mortar positions, artillery and armour in Kosovo with RBL755s and eight aircraft targeted Serbian troops in dug-in positions with a mix of CBUs and 1000-lb bombs. During this period, there were also aircraft that were held in orbits but were not given any targets by AFACs. For the next week, around 20 Harrier sorties were launched each day from Gioia del Colle. Pilots targeted Serbian forces, concentrating particularly on artillery and mortar positions.

The 20 Harrier sorties flown on 3 June included pairs led by Flt Lt Garland and Sqn Ldr Ball. After arriving in their holding pattern over Albania, Garland chopped across to the strike frequency and heard an AFAC working a target two kilometres north of Dakovica that required CBUs. The Harriers answered the call and were directed to two APCs in revetments, which they bombed, with Flt Lt Zanker in the No 2 aircraft scoring a hit on the southerly vehicle.

Meanwhile, an A-10 AFAC tasked Sqn Ldr Ball and Flt Lt Averty against a complex of eight artillery emplacements near a village. Two of the positions were attacked, but the airburst bombs dropped short of the aiming point and one of them detonated prematurely. Concerned at the fate of the nearby village, the Harrier pilots subsequently checked their TIALD footage and were relieved to find that the houses were unscathed; they had in fact hit two other artillery positions.

Harrier sorties continued apace over the following four days, with a mix of CAS and armed reconnaissance missions. The last sorties of Operation *Engadine*/*Allied Force* were flown on 7 June, and these 20 missions concluded the campaign against Serbian artillery and mortar units. On their last CAS sortie, Flt Lts Zanker and Earl also had the novelty of working with a US Navy AFAC crew in an F-14 Tomcat that directed them against artillery positions near Kosovska Mitrovica.

A ceasefire was declared on 10 June, after which the NATO-led multi-national peacekeeping Kosovo Force moved in. However, tensions still ran high, as Flt Lt Zanker described;

'The UK ground forces moved into Kosovo from the south and Russian forces moved in from the north, causing significant tension and a race to get to Pristina airfield. The army wanted 24-hour CAS cover. It was decided that we would need to fly low-level night CAS missions, and we were a little out of practice. At the beginning of June pilots were rotated back to Wittering to fly one day low-level sortie followed by one night low-level sortie. Back at Gioia, we then spent many days and nights effectively on QRA [quick reaction alert]. Thankfully, we weren't needed.'

The Harrier GR 7 detachment had flown 870 operational sorties during the course of Operation *Engadine*. The experience had been useful in identifying the limitations of laser-guided bombs, particularly in poor weather conditions, and led to the development of the Enhanced Paveway II weapon which could also be dropped using the target GPS coordinates. With hostilities over, most of the RAF aircraft in-theatre were withdrawn during the summer of 1999, leaving six Harrier GR 7s at Gioia del Colle and two TriStars at Ancona. By July, No 3 Sqn was responsible for manning the Harrier detachment at Gioia del Colle.

CHAPTER FIVE

IRAQ

Four Harrier GR 7s fly along the coast of Sinai on 23 January 2003 on their way to Ahmed al-Jaber air base in Kuwait in preparation for Operation *Telic*. These aircraft formed the first wave of the Harrier deployment for the impending campaign, and they were supported by a TriStar tanker of No 216 Sqn (*Andrew Suddards*)

OPERATION *TELIC*

Since Operation *Bolton* in 1997–98, the relationship between the UN and Iraq had deteriorated markedly, and by late 2002 it was obvious that there would be further conflict in the Gulf region. Preparations began for an invasion of Iraq, and particular emphasis was placed on neutralising its Tactical Ballistic Missile (TBM) capability. During Gulf War I in 1991, Iraqi R-17 Elbrus (Scud B) TBMs deployed in the western desert of Iraq had threatened Israel and other neighbouring countries.

The missiles themselves were extremely dangerous and their launcher systems had proved to be elusive, so the USAF's Air Combat Command had devised a counter-TBM strategy in case of further hostilities. The plan entailed reconnaissance and offensive support aircraft working closely with SF teams on the ground, and included RAF assets like the Harriers of No 3 Sqn. The unit had started a work-up for the counter-TBM role in late 2002, undertaking two deployments to the Nellis AFB ranges in Nevada to perfect and practise the techniques for hunting and destroying the Iraqi TBM systems. As a result, No 3 Sqn established a very close working relationship with both the USAF counter-TBM forces and SF troops.

The large-scale deployment of Coalition forces into the Gulf theatre which commenced in early 2003 saw the establishment of detachments of RAF combat aircraft in Saudi Arabia, Kuwait and Qatar. The original plan

was for 12 Harrier GR 7s from Nos 1 and 4 Sqns to operate from Batman air base in eastern Turkey to support ground forces, and for six Harriers from No 3 Sqn to deploy to Azraq (Muwaffaq Salti air base), in Jordan, for counter-TBM operations in the western desert of Iraq. However, the Turkish government would not allow air operations to be carried out from its bases, so the main force of 12 Harriers went to Ahmad al-Jaber air base in Kuwait on 23 February 2003 instead. Here, they formed Harrier Force South under the command of Wg Cdr Suddards. At the same time, the counter-TBM force at Azraq was enlarged to nine aircraft to form Harrier Force West under the command of Wg Cdr Atha.

Led by Wg Cdr Suddards, the aircraft destined for Harrier Force South left Cottesmore for Akrotiri on 22 February, arriving in-theatre the following day. After a couple of false starts, the main party travelled by RAF TriStar, landing at Kuwait International Airport on the night of 24–25 February. 'I will never forget the scenes as we left the TriStar', remarked Flt Lt I J Townsend, one of the QWIs on No 1 Sqn. 'It was still hot, despite being night, and the airfield had a strange orange glow from numerous lights. The glow illuminated more military kit and personnel than I had ever seen in one place. Aircraft, armoured fighting vehicles, Patriot missile systems and lots and lots of people. It was an electric atmosphere, and any doubts that we would leave without fighting were immediately dispelled. You simply don't mass this level of military capability without using it'.

Ahmad al-Jaber air base, home to the US Marines Expeditionary Force (MEF), was no less busy. The initial Harrier sorties from here, flown between 27 February and 6 March both in daylight and at night, were area familiarisation flights for the pilots within the Kuwait Military Operating Areas. Each pilot flew four such sorties before being qualified to fly into

A Harrier GR 7 at Ahmed al-Jaber air base prepares to taxi out for an Operation *Telic* mission over Iraq. The aircraft is loaded with two 1000-lb Paveway II LGBs and two RBL755 cluster bombs, and it also carries a TIALD pod under the fuselage. With a mixed weapon load such as this, the pilot could respond to any request from a FAC (*Crown Copyright/MoD*)

A view through NVGs of a Harrier GR 7 over Iraq during Operation *Telic*. Many of the Harrier sorties early in the campaign were carried out at night, using the nocturnal capability of the aeroplane – the cockpit of the Harrier GR 7 was fully compatible with NVGs (*Crown Copyright/MoD*)

Iraq itself. Flt Lt Townsend flew his first familiarisation sortie on 1 March, later writing;

'My last sortie had been a night flight in the UK, during which I had suffered a generator failure and had had to divert from the Lake District into Newcastle airport. My first sortie in Kuwait was similarly "interesting", resulting in my first and last Mayday call of my military flying career. As I approached the circuit to land, the audio warning sounded. Looking down, I saw something that was incredibly unusual – a double Electronic Fuel Computer failure (the Red and the Green cautions). The ramifications were potentially very serious – e.g. the total loss of engine control. I selected manual fuel system and got the jet on the ground ASAP. All uneventful, but an interesting way to arrive at the end of Sortie One.

'What the first sortie also demonstrated was the enormity of what was going on at al-Jaber. A concrete factory had been in place for weeks, enabling the creation of seemingly endless aircraft dispersals. More than 200 combat aircraft were now gathered, and whilst taxiing out on that first daytime sortie, I remember being awed by the collection of different aircraft types and the sheer scale of air power at this one location. And it was busy, day and night. An endless stream of aircraft taxiing, departing, recovering. Simply awesome.'

Since Operation *Southern Watch* was still ongoing in the Southern NFZ over Iraq, the initial sorties into Iraq were tasked for that operation. Wg Cdr Suddards flew on the first of these missions on 7 March, and further Operation *Southern Watch* missions were undertaken over the next ten days. The aircraft were flown in pairs, and sortie lengths were typically around 1 hr 20 min. On some sorties the Harriers practised strike coordination and reconnaissance tactics with USAF A-10s.

Meanwhile, planning was already underway for the missions that would take place once hostilities commenced. 'On 17 March I received the first targeting pack for "Night 1"', recalled Flt Lt Townsend. 'This was extraordinarily exciting and, as the lead QWI, I set about putting together a plan which saw a mix of GPS- and laser-guided weapons employed by a four-ship. It was an exquisite plan, with all eventualities considered. Amazingly, on 18 March, I led a four-ship which practised the very attack we would conduct on "Night 1". The plan worked well and I had no doubt it would be a success when the word came.

'And then, on 20 March, the war started, and, as has been widely reported, it all happened quite quickly. In fact, by the time I reported to work, the target I had planned and recce'd on 18 March was now inside Coalition territory, highlighting how quickly our land forces had progressed in a short space of time. But it had started, and we were off.'

Armed Harriers under sun shelters at Ahmed al-Jaber air base. The HAS from which this photograph was taken was still unusable after being damaged during the first Gulf War 12 years previously. This image also illustrates the reduced visibility, due to sand and dust in the air, that affected missions early in the campaign (*Crown Copyright/MoD*)

For Harrier Force West, hostilities had started at 1800 hrs GMT on 19 March when six aircraft led by Wg Cdr Atha began providing overwatch for SF teams as they crossed the border into Iraq and pushed into the desert. It was a long sortie – just short of nine hours of night flying, involving five AAR brackets with a TriStar tanker. Poor weather hampered air operations on 20 March, but the next day aircraft from Harrier Force West each spent more than four hours patrolling Highway 10 – the main road between Baghdad and Amman. Wg Cdr Atha located Iraqi vehicles parked near a Roland SAM battery.

Meanwhile, Harrier Force South also had a busy day on 21 March providing CAS for the US Marine Corps and 40 Commando Royal Marines as they advanced into the al-Faw peninsula. Daylight sorties included the destruction of an Iraqi artillery piece by Wg Cdr Suddards with an Enhanced Paveway II, while Flt Lt Townsend and his wingman worked with a FAC near Tallil to attack six Iraqi APCs using IR AGM-65G2 Maverick air-to-ground missiles.

'I flew mostly at night as one of the more experienced pilots, which I absolutely loved', Townsend explained. 'I almost smile when I recall the US chaplain who would stand at the exit of the aircraft dispersal holding a luminous green crucifix blessing each of us as we taxied past! There are many things I recall vividly. The stream of headlights of Coalition forces snaking their way out of Kuwait and every night making more and more progress into Iraq, the challenge of finding the refuellers at night with only a lat/long and time and no radar to help the silent comms join up, and the endless bursts of light as some brave Iraqi air defence unit tried to bring down one of our aircraft. It was an awesome thing to be a part of.

'We also got a feel for how we could be more successful in our missions. Some missions were tasked against specific targets, but mostly we were standing by whilst airborne, waiting for someone to need us for CAS, or we were left to find our own targets. This latter task required a degree of cunning and ingenuity. We would firstly try and work in the MEF area to the east of Iraq, where the US Marine Corps was far more prepared

The Raytheon AGM-65G2 Maverick air-to-surface missile had been procured after the Kosovo campaign, where the limitations of the RBL755 had become apparent. This version of the missile used an IR sensor for guidance. During Operation *Telic*, some 38 Mavericks were fired by Harriers (*Crown Copyright/MoD*)

and familiar with allowing aircraft to conduct attacks near its own troops without the need for close coordination (in other words, CAS). We would also visit the MEF HQ [at Ahmad al-Jaber air base], which had a system that would tell us where enemy comms had been detected in the previous few hours so that we could make a fair guess of where they might be. Once airborne, we had a choice of weapons to use once we found the enemy.'

As well as CRV7 rockets and 1000- and 540-lb freefall bombs, the Harriers were armed with AGM-65G2 Maverick missiles and new Enhanced Paveway II LGBs that could also be dropped accurately on to GPS coordinates if laser guidance was not practical.

The first Maverick to be launched operationally from a Harrier GR 7 was fired by Flt Lt M F Rutland of No 4 Sqn on the afternoon of 21 March. He was No 2 in a pair of Harriers operating 200 miles into southern Iraq when the formation was re-tasked to attack a mobile SAM launcher that had been detected moving across the desert. 'It was hard to see. It was moving very fast, swerving and then slowing up', reported Rutland, adding 'my main thought was that I don't mess this up!' The missile, fired from medium-level, scored a direct hit on the vehicle.

With most of the TIALD pods allocated to Harrier Force West for the counter-TBM missions, the number available at Ahmad al-Jaber air base for Harrier Force South was limited. Nevertheless, with careful programming and hard work by the groundcrews, there was generally one TIALD pod fitted to the leader of each pair of aircraft. In this way, leaders could self-designate their own weapons and cooperatively designate for the wingman.

'My busiest night', recalled Flt Lt Townsend, 'came on 27 March, when we worked with a Tornado GR 4 formation [from Ali Al Salem air base in Kuwait] to target an enemy APC convoy. This was the first night where

I came home "Winchester", with all stores expended – two Enhanced Paveway IIs and two 540-lb freefall bombs, and I also spiked my wingman's weapons in. Professionally, very rewarding'.

While Harrier Force South was busy supporting the main Coalition thrust towards Baghdad, their colleagues in Harrier Force West were participating in the counter-TBM campaign in the western desert. Mobile SF teams were scouring the terrain for Scud launchers and patrolling the highways to stop the Iraqi army from using them as deployment or resupply routes. Pairs of Harriers were part of the continuous presence of offensive support aircraft overhead the area, ready to respond to any call from the SF teams for CAS. Here again, air operations were restricted by the weather conditions, and much of the flying was limited to low-level, where the aircraft became vulnerable to ground defences such as AAA and SAMs.

Nevertheless, the Harriers were frequently called to strike Iraqi ground forces, often in close proximity to SF teams. AAR tankers enabled the aircraft to remain on station for as long as possible. In contrast to the missions flown by Harrier Force South, which were typically between one-and-a-half to two-and-a-half hours in duration, the Harriers flying from Azraq were generally flying four- to five-hour sorties.

Responding to a task from AWACS during a six-hour sortie on 23 March, Wg Cdr Atha and Flt Lt S A Berry prepared to attack four guard posts at a water treatment facility at Al-Qaim, but by the time they obtained clearance to release their weapons from the SF team on the ground, they were running short of fuel and handed the task over to the next pair of Harriers led by Sqn Ldr Mounsey. The following night thick cloud extending from low-level up to 31,000 ft curtailed operations over the western desert.

The tasking for Harrier Force South was typically for Kill-box Interdiction CAS (KI/CAS), a US Marine Corps concept whereby Iraq was divided up into discrete 'kill-boxes', each measuring 30 miles by 30 miles. If aircraft were tasked into an 'open' kill-box, they could attack any targets

From its position in front of a damaged HAS, a Harrier GR 7 armed with a pair of 1000-lb Paveway II LGBs and equipped with a TIALD pod prepares to taxi for a mission over Iraq. Since most of the TIALD pods had been allocated to Harrier Force West, where they were needed for counter-TBM operations, aircraft from Harrier Force South generally flew with one pod per pair of aircraft (*Crown Copyright/MoD*)

Groundcrew servicing a Maverick-armed Harrier GR 7 during Operation *Telic*. The aircraft is also carrying a freefall bomb on the centreline pylon. Note the BOL chaff magazines on the ground in front of the wing, these being fitted on to the front of the AAM rails (*Crown Copyright/MoD*)

such as military vehicles that they found in the area. If it was a 'closed' kill-box, the crew would be controlled by a FAC on to specific targets.

The capability of the Harrier GR 7 to attack point targets was further improved a few days into the conflict with the arrival in-theatre of the electro-optically-guided TV Maverick. The IR Maverick was very effective at night when the temperature contrast between the target and its surroundings was well-defined, but in the heat of the day, the IR signature of the target frequently merged with its background. On the other hand, TV Maverick, which used the visible light spectrum, could detect targets in daylight more easily, although it could not be used at night. The Enhanced Paveway II also continued to be both flexible and accurate as a precision weapon.

'I recall the mission on 30 March vividly', wrote Flt Lt Townsend. 'Tasked to refuel and then proceed to conduct "XCAS" airborne alert overhead Baghdad, which was still the heart of the Iraqi defensive system – our Intelligence Officers were briefing us daily on the status of the Super-MEZ [Missile Engagement Zone]. It was very much alive and well. So, with a degree of trepidation, we set off for Baghdad. It was a clear night, with the same vista of our Coalition marching steadily northwards.

'Perhaps fortuitously, we were re-tasked to attack a communications mast south of the capital (and outside of the Super-MEZ). My wingman and I had worked together on the earlier attack at Tallil, and we had a good relationship. We quickly reworked our route to the comms mast and prepared the attack, which consisted of three runs – two single Enhanced Paveway IIs (spiked by myself) to see what effect we would have on this relatively large structure, followed by a single attack with two Enhanced Paveway IIs that I would self-designate.

'All the attacks worked perfectly, and I subsequently learnt that we were successful in disrupting comms from the facility. I also learnt almost immediately after the first attack that there were some folk on the ground who clearly weren't chuffed about our plan, and the sky lit up with small arms tracer.'

The end of March also marked the switch over to predominantly daylight operations, although some night missions continued to be flown. Wg Cdr Suddards and Sqn Ldr Provost flew a four-hour night mission on 1 April, during which they dropped Enhanced Paveway IIs on enemy forces near Ramallah.

To the west of Baghdad, the US-led Task Force 20 (TF-20) had seized the Haditha Dam, but it was being pressed by Iraqi troops armed with mortars and artillery. Wg Cdr Atha and Flt Lt J A A Schofield supported TF-20 on 2 April, the former dropping an Enhanced Paveway II on an artillery position, designated by a FAC, while the latter fired a Maverick at the same target. The pilots then attacked Iraqi troops that were threatening the TF-20 team.

The next day, the same pair were tasked to support a SF team near Ar-Rutbah. Again, the main target was an artillery emplacement, but the attack was complicated by the proximity of a mosque just 200 m away. Atha decided not to fire a Maverick in case it might cause collateral damage to the mosque, but Schofield was able to drop Enhanced Paveway IIs that were designated by a FAC who was located on a hilltop to the south of the town.

On 5 April battles were still raging near the Haditha Dam, and a TF-20 FAC requested that Wg Cdr Atha and Flt Lt M T Lalley drop Enhanced Paveway IIs on to buildings in Haditha village that

were being used as strongpoints by Iraqi forces. Atha noted that the 'US SF were v[ery] happy with the support'. By 7 April, the situation in the area was much calmer, and Harriers from Azraq were tasked with overwatch of a convoy of some 30 vehicles, including ten M-1 Abrams tanks, as it made its way from H-1 air base, in Anbar Province, across the Haditha Dam and on towards Tikrit. At the end of his four-hour stint, Wg Cdr Atha handed over responsibility for the overwatch to Sqn Ldr H Smyth. Shortly afterwards, an SA-9 SAM was fired at Smyth, who successfully evaded the missile – a US tank quickly accounted for the launch vehicle.

By the end of the second week of operations, Coalition forces had reached the outskirts of Baghdad. The tasking for Harrier Force South continued to consist of KI/CAS kill-boxes across the country. Aircraft were directed to kill-boxes to the south and west of Baghdad, as well as in the Basra area. On 2 April, Flt Lt Townsend was sent to a kill-box south of

Sqn Ldr Ned Cullen (right) and Flt Lt Al Allsop undertook the mission during which Harrier Force West achieved 1000 hours flying from Azraq. Sqn Ldr Cullen had developed a very close working relationship with the USAF, and his major part in planning the air campaign in the Western Desert was recognised with the awarding of an MBE. Unfortunately, he was later diagnosed with motor neurone disease (*Stuart Atha*)

Decorated with a 'sharksmouth' on the nose, Harrier GR 7 ZD408 from Harrier Force South flies over central Baghdad just days after the ceasefire. During the conflict Baghdad was protected by a Super-MEZ containing numerous SAM batteries, and flying through the middle of it was not recommended. ZD408 was destroyed in a non-fatal crash near Cottesmore on 16 June 2008 after the engine seized and caught fire following the loss of its oil (*Andrew Suddards*)

al-Amarah, where he bombed vehicles in high-sided berms with Enhanced Paveway II. By 8 April, the Harriers were being mainly employed on armed reconnaissance missions as there were few CAS targets remaining.

On 9 April Sqn Ldr A J E Cullen and Flt Lt A J Allsop flew the mission during which Harrier Force West achieved its 1000th operational flying hour since the conflict had begun. Four days later, the ground war was largely over. In all, Harrier Force West flew 290 sorties during the campaign, releasing 73 weapons during 32 sorties. Over the same period, Harrier Force South flew 389 operational missions between 21 March and 14 April, during which 117 weapons were expended. Some 22 reconnaissance missions were also flown from Ahmed al-Jaber air base using the Digital Joint Reconnaissance Pod (DJRP).

The air operations over Iraq during Operation *Telic* were remarkable in that 85 per cent of the weapons expended (by both Harrier and Tornado) were Precision-Guided Munitions, as compared to just ten per cent during the 1991 Gulf War. In addition, many of the CAS missions flown by Harrier Force West had been 'danger close' – in other words, against enemy forces that were in contact with friendly forces – and these sorties had been performed successfully without causing any blue-on-blue casualties

Furthermore, a measure of the success of the counter-TBM campaign in the western desert is that despite an intensive search of the area, not a single Scud launcher was found. As Sqn Ldr Smyth explained, 'we put so much effort into finding the missiles that we created the effect desired and scared them off'.

CHAPTER SIX

AFGHANISTAN

On 11 September 2001, al-Qaeda terrorists flew hijacked airliners into the World Trade Center in New York City and the Pentagon in Washington, D.C. In response to these attacks, US armed forces commenced operations in Afghanistan to remove the threat posed by al-Qaeda and the Islamist Taliban government in the country. US aircraft started offensive operations over Afghanistan on 9 October 2001, but at that stage the British participation was limited to the provision of AAR support to US Navy aircraft operating from carriers sailing in the Arabian Sea. By December, an agreement had been reached by the UN to establish an International Security Assistance Force (ISAF) in Afghanistan.

At the end of 2003, NATO took responsibility for the ISAF in Afghanistan, and the British military presence in the country, codenamed Operation *Herrick*, was increased accordingly. Six Harrier GR 7As from No 3 Sqn deployed to Kandahar Air Field (KAF) on 24 September 2004 for what was intended to be a nine-month detachment to provide CAS for ISAF troops.

The more powerful GR 7A variant was sent to Afghanistan because of the 'hot and high' conditions at Kandahar, particularly in the summer months. As Sqn Ldr I Townsend put it, 'this was the perfect operation for the Harrier GR 7A. The big engine provided the "grunt" required to easily manage operations from an airfield which was more than 3000 ft above sea level, and the aircraft could easily climb to, and operate

Although it is not obvious from the 'fleet number', this is actually a Harrier GR 7A flying over the mountains of central Afghanistan. The white canister on the underwing pylon is a CRV7 'training pod', which contains six rockets. The store on the missile rail is an AIM-9L acquisition round, which would normally be used for training missions, but in this case is fitted to counterbalance a heavier store under the right wing – probably a CRV7 operational pod containing 19 rockets (*Crown Copyright/MoD*) above, 30,000 ft – ideal when conducting reconnaissance missions above 18,000-ft mountains north of Kabul.

'The VSTOL capabilities of the jet were essential at KAF. After each take off, the runway would disintegrate due to the poor Soviet design (one-inch tarmac and then simply a layer of gravel). This meant that our first jet would take off from the threshold, almost certainly damaging the runway at the "STO point" (where the nozzles were rotated for launch). The second jet would then enter the runway at a point after the damage and do what the Harrier did so well – short take-offs.

'Once airborne, any available squadron personnel would be stood next to the runway with brushes ready to sweep the gravel back into the holes caused by the departing Harriers and remove any massive chunks of runway (of which there were plenty). Once this task had been completed, a tarmac lorry would appear, fill the hole, flatten the surface and wait for the jets to return two hours later, at which point the runway was good enough to use again. Perfect expeditionary operations!

'Take-off was always a lot of fun. Stay low and fast until speed was sufficient to perform a zoom climb, avoiding the gaze of the enemy (and their missile systems) for as long as possible. Equally, the recovery demanded an arrival at height and a spiral descent to land, rather than our tradition "run in and break". Again, the VSTOL capabilities of the aircraft allowed a tight spiralling descent with plenty of nozzle and a last minute "nozzle out", flare and touch down.'

Over the following months, the other Harrier GR 7 units each took their turn for a four-month tour of duty at Kandahar, with No 1 Sqn following No 3 Sqn in January 2005 and then No 4 Sqn taking over in April. Although the deployment had been due to end in July, it was extended initially to the end of August 2005 and then to June 2006, based on the need to cover the period of runway work at Kandahar. A subsequent further extension to 'at least 31 March 2007' reflected the fact that the Harrier detachment had by then become a vital part of Operation *Herrick* in the face of an increased Taliban insurgency.

In late 2004, a plan had been hatched to change over two aircraft at Kandahar in early 2005 by flying replacement jets in directly from the flightdeck of a carrier. The task was given to No 3 Sqn just after it had participated in Exercise Magic Carpet in Oman. As dawn broke on 3 March 2005, a pair of Harriers from the unit, flown by Wg Cdr A Offer and Sqn Ldr Townsend launched from *Invincible* in the Indian Ocean and transited through Pakistani airspace at 25,000 ft.

'As transit flights go, this was epic', commented Townsend. 'Pakistan was simply stunning, made more so by a rising sun and azure blue skies as the sun rose. There was nothing to do really except enjoy the view and prepare for the arrival at Kandahar. My first look at Kandahar again remains fixed in the memory. To the southwest, a deep red desert, to the west, greenery in what would become known as the Green Zone (in and around Helmand Province), and to the north, the land simply continued to rise beyond Afghanistan, through the Hindu Kush and onwards to the Himalayas.

'But around Kandahar were ominous looking clouds, and the blue skies of Pakistan had given way to some unfavourable weather. As I

The view from the Harrier GR 7 cockpit of Sqn Ldr 'Cab' Townsend upon entering Afghanistan for the first time on 3 March 2005, having launched from *Invincible* in the Arabian Sea at dawn. The lead aircraft can be seen ahead and to the left (*Ian Townsend*)

would learn during my four months in Afghanistan (February to April and November to December 2005), it rains and, when it does, it rains hard. What I didn't realise was that I was now approaching the most alarming landing I would ever have in a Harrier (and that is saying something noting the V/STOL tomfoolery many of us engaged in as our experience built).

'In close formation, receiving a Precision Approach Radar from Kandahar tower, we broke through cloud at about 1000 ft, at which point I dropped back to give myself some separation from the Boss on landing. Wg Cdr Offer touched down, and a plume of vapour rose from around his aircraft – a familiar sight for any Harrier landing or take off in the wet. I touched down and waited for my speed to reduce to 80 knots before applying the brakes . . . and absolutely nothing happened. The runway was wet, and this was no ordinary runway. Being a relic from the Soviet Union, it had none of the friction qualities we insist on in the West. It was worse than landing on packed snow in Norway, and I had no retardation.

'In any other jet, this would be an issue, but, of course, I still had the nozzle lever to stop me from colliding with the Boss, who was becoming increasingly large in my canopy. Braking stop was applied and I introduced a whole heap of power to slow down. I remember doing this at Linton-on-Ouse [in North Yorkshire] during my Harrier OCU [Operational Conversion Unit] course and, being in a light jet at the end of the sortie, in my enthusiasm I applied too much power and got airborne again . . . in the braking stop, triggering activation of the ATC [air traffic control] crash alarm by a concerned controller (who happened to be a pal of mine from officer training)! This time, the Paveways, fuel tanks and being at an altitude of 3300 ft meant my enthusiastic application of power achieved the desired results. I slowed, and we taxied in to the Harrier dispersal. Phew.

'Quick turn, a quick brief (and it was a really quick brief, despite the fact I'd not flown missions in Afghanistan previously), and I was now following an old friend on my first operational mission, conducting CAS in and around Musa Qal'eh. Admiring the landscape and historic fort of Musa Qal'eh, the 1 hr 25 min mission passed quickly, and soon we were back at Kandahar, which was still wet, but I was now prepared for the ice rink ahead.

'Another quick turn and I was at the controls of my third jet of the day, which was to take me back to *Invincible*. But all was not well. My aircraft was having issues and time was ticking away to get airborne and return to the ship before our [already extended] crew duty expired. I really didn't want to stay overnight at Kandahar in a wet and cold tent, with no booze, when my toasty cabin, wardroom and clean clothes seemed like a much better option. But there was no need to worry, for the engineering team came good and the Boss and I were airborne and heading back to *Invincible* for "tea and medals", having launched the ship and No 3 Sqn's first operational missions into Afghanistan. However, things were strangely quiet once we landed . . . eerily quiet.

'Whilst I wasn't expecting a marching band and handshakes from all, this was a pretty significant achievement and deserved something. What we didn't know was that earlier in the day, a Royal Navy Lynx had launched from *Invincible* and ditched before the helicopter could reach its ship, HMS *Nottingham*. All the Lynx aircrew survived, and one of them was in the wardroom when Wg Cdr Offer and I arrived for a well-deserved beer – and it's fair to say, he looked like he'd had a much worse day than us.'

The role of the Harrier in Afghanistan was threefold – firstly CAS, secondly airborne Intelligence, Surveillance and Reconnaissance, and thirdly the provision of 'air presence patrols'. This latter task was part of the ISAF support for the security of the Afghan presidential elections in October 2004.

The initial routine tasking for the Harriers was for day missions, and since the aircraft were Coalition, rather than exclusively British, air assets, their area of operations stretched as far as the borders with Pakistan, Iran, Turkmenistan and Uzbekistan. Pre-planned sorties might involve overwatch of convoys or army units, as well as reconnaissance sorties using the DJRP. Pilots could also be diverted from any task to respond to a Troops In Contact (TIC) incident where CAS was needed. In practice, there was little pre-planning that could be done for CAS sorties, and it became increasingly the norm for Harrier pilots to take off from Kandahar with little idea of where they might be going or what they might be expected to do when they got there.

On operational sorties, the Harriers flew in pairs both for mutual support and to allow a wide range of weaponry to be carried. Throughout the day, another pair of aircraft also maintained GCAS alert, ready to launch within 15 minutes to respond to short-notice emergency tasking. Sqn Ldr Townsend stated that 'most of those who flew from Kandahar would remember GCAS most fondly. Sat on alert in flying kit, the "Scramble" call would be accompanied by an old-fashioned rotary fire bell . . . literally a scene from the Battle of Britain.

'Scramble would set heart beats immediately racing as the two pilots raced to the Land Rover parked outside our wooden ops shed, start up

Harrier GR 7A ZD408 releases decoy flares as it banks away over Afghanistan during an Operation *Herrick* mission. The aircraft is armed with 1000-lb Paveway II LGBs and carries a TIALD pod under the fuselage. Since there was no air-to-air threat over Afghanistan, there was no requirement to carry self-defence missiles, but there was extra protection against radar-directed SAMs in the form of additional BOL missile rails (*Ian Townsend*)

and roar down the taxiway (no comms with ATC needed, for we were the only ones operating on that side of the airfield) and dash to our jets a mile-and-a-half away. Prepped with as many switches "made" as possible, and life jackets and helmets hanging off the pylons, all we needed to do was jump into the cockpit, strap in, start and go. Twelve minutes was my personal best, and, in hindsight, I cannot believe we got airborne so quickly and safely.

'The very best thing about a GCAS scramble was the knowledge that at the other end of the radio was someone who required our help. Establishing comms with the FAC, the sound of machine gun fire and tension in their voices told you everything you needed to know about their need for help. Of all my operational sorties, those flown in the assistance of troops in TIC situations in Afghanistan were the most rewarding. Real "Boys' Own" stuff, and an adrenaline rush like no other.'

Within each pair, the aircraft carried a different weapon load so as to give the maximum mission flexibility. Generally, one Harrier would be loaded with two 540-lb freefall bombs that had the option of airburst or impact fusing and two pods of CRV7 rockets. One would be a 'training pod' containing six rockets, while the other would be a full warshot of 19 rounds. This aircraft also carried a DJRP. The other Harrier would be configured with a TIALD pod, one 1000-lb freefall bomb and an Enhanced Paveway II LGB.

Although weapons were carried from the start of Operation *Herrick*, there was only one bomb release in the first six months of the deployment. Quoted in *Flight* magazine in April 2006, Flt Lt I M Bews of No 1 Sqn

In order to change the engine in a Harrier, the wing had to be removed. Here, Air Engineering Technicians from 800 NAS are undertaking an engine change on a Harrier GR 7 in a temporary hangar at Kandahar air base in October 2006 (*Crown Copyright/ MoD*)

reckoned that 'nine times out of ten, noise on the ground is all we need, but if we need a Show of Force [SOF], we come in at 100 ft'. In a SOF, one aircraft would carry out a low-level high-speed flypast of the enemy position while the other remained high above providing overwatch. Apart from the shock of the noise, the SOF demonstrated that a fully armed aeroplane was on station, and that it would shortly be deploying its powerful weaponry if the enemy forces did not withdraw. Frequently, that had sufficient deterrent effect to break any contact with friendly forces.

When directly supporting Coalition troops, the aircraft were invariably controlled by FACs, which were now known by the American term Joint Terminal Attack Controllers (JTACs). Sorties over Afghanistan typically lasted between one and two hours, but they might be extended beyond three hours with AAR support.

As the detachment progressed and the Taliban insurgency gathered strength, the number of 'kinetic events' where weapons were employed increased. There were ten such events between April and September 2005, but by the time that the 1000th mission had been flown in late April 2006 there had already been ten more weapon drops, and there was about to be an exponential rise in the frequency of kinetic events.

The tasking for Harrier GR 7As increased dramatically in the spring of 2006 when Britain took over responsibility for the security of Helmand Province in the southwest of the country. At this point the British task changed, as an Army report later put it, from a military operation into a war. Reflecting the increased need for CAS at night, the Harrier detachment started to operate two pairs by day and a pair at night.

The move into Helmand was countered by a major increase in the Taliban insurgency in the area, for this had recently been one of their strongholds. The Taliban was also active around Kandahar, and periodically carried out rocket attacks against the air base. A salvo fired by insurgents on 14 October 2005 badly damaged two Harrier GR 7As. One aircraft (ZD408) was repairable on site, but the other (ZD469) was recovered to Britain, where it was deemed to have been damaged beyond economic repair.

No 3 Sqn had taken over the Harrier detachment at Kandahar for the last time between July and October 2005, prior to its re-equipment with the Typhoon F 2 the following April. At that point its aircraft were transferred to the newly-reformed 800 NAS of the Fleet Air Arm, which took its place in the JFH.

Between October and December 2005, the Kandahar detachment was manned by No 4 Sqn, which was followed in turn by No 1 Sqn from January 2006 until the following May. Then No 4 Sqn, now commanded by Wg Cdr I W Duguid, took over once again between May and September 2006. By this time the detachment had been enlarged to eight aircraft and the operational tempo had begun to pick up noticeably – Harriers were called in to fly SOFs or to employ weapons on a regular basis.

For example, Harriers provided CAS for troops in contact with enemy forces near Gereshk and Musah Qal'eh on 6 July and again near Kandahar and Musah Qal'eh the next day. On 9 July, the Harriers joined USAF A-10s and *Armée de l'Air* Mirage 2000s for CAS to troops in contact near Kandahar. Then, the following week, they were in action again near Now Zad on 22 July and Musah Qal'eh on 23 July. During the latter mission, they worked with Mirage 2000s supporting ISAF troops who had been

A fully armed Harrier GR 7 at readiness in a sun shelter at Kandahar air base. Two aircraft were continuously held at readiness for GCAS, and the pilots were ready to be airborne within 15 minutes to respond to the needs of Coalition ground forces (*Ian Townsend*)

ambushed and were taking small arms and rocket-propelled grenade fire from the Taliban. The Harriers engaged the enemy with CRV7 rockets and a 540-lb bomb.

More CRV7s were fired at Taliban positions near Lashkar Gah on 29 July, and CRV7s and a 540-lb bomb were expended near Musah Qal'eh on 2 August. The next day saw another engagement near Kandahar, during which A-10s, Mirage 2000s and a B-1B were also involved, and Harrier GR 7As fired CRV7s and dropped an Enhanced Paveway II. Working again with a B-1B on 8 August, Harriers supported Coalition troops in contact with Taliban forces near Musah Qal'eh, dropping a 1000-lb bomb and an Enhanced Paveway II on to a Taliban mortar position. Meanwhile, other Harriers provided CAS at a TIC incident near Tarin Kowt, although in this case there was no need to expend any weapons.

Further CAS missions in support of ISAF troops under fire were flown on 10 August near Oruzgan, on 18 August near Musah Qal'eh and in the vicinity of Qalat and on 21 August close to Tarin Kowt. Sqn Ldr D Killeen also reported that 'there have been engagements against aircraft, isolated engagements, whilst low flying – small arms, rocket-propelled grenades, small rockets. We haven't suffered any damage [yet, but] there are man-portable air defences in-theatre, definitely, and there are also AAA systems known to be on the ground in Helmand'.

The pace of operations continued to accelerate, and in September alone, the Harrier detachment flew almost 250 sorties and dropped almost 70 bombs, including Enhanced Paveway II LGBs and 540- and 1000-lb freefall bombs. More than 400 CRV7 rockets were also expended.

During the first half of the month, the Canadian-led Operation *Medusa* sought to drive the Taliban out of Kandahar Province. The operation was particularly hard fought near Kandahar on 7 and 8 September. On the first of these days, a pair of Harriers, coordinated with A-10s, supported ISAF troops and fired CRV7 rockets that successfully forced the Taliban to withdraw from their location. In a separate incident, Harriers dropped 540-lb bombs to bring a TIC to a close. On the 8th, the Harriers worked with US Navy F/A-18s to bring Taliban resistance from one firing position to an end by expending CRV7s and dropping an Enhanced Paveway II LGB. Later that same day, Harriers again fired CRV7s in support of ISAF troops.

On 21 September the Harriers worked with AV-8Bs of the US Marine Corps near Garmsir (35 miles south of Lashkar Gar), firing CRV7s and dropping a 540-lb bomb on Taliban positions, while the AV-8Bs expended a GBU-12 and a GBU-38.

800 NAS, commanded by Cdr A P Orchard, had spent the summer completing its operational work-up, including conducting its first deployment on board *Illustrious* as part of Exercise Magic Carpet 06 in Oman. At the end of September 2006, it was the turn of 800 NAS to take over from No 4 Sqn at Kandahar. This changeover occurred as the Taliban insurgency was reaching its peak activity.

Sqn Ldr D C Mason, who had already completed an operational deployment at Kandahar with No 1 Sqn in March 2006, commented that 'the situation had changed completely since my first deployment.

In March there might have been two or three kinetic events during the whole detachment. Now, it was almost two or three events every day!' By the end of October, 800 NAS pilots had dropped more than 32,000 lbs of bombs, which was more than No 4 Sqn had expended during the entire previous detachment. Harrier missions included providing CAS near Now Zad on 3 October, during which they worked with US Navy F/A-18s and dropped an Enhanced Paveway II LGB, and again on 6 October, when a 540-lb bomb was dropped on Taliban positions in the same area, with CRV7s being fired during a TIC event near Now Zad on the 7th.

The Harriers also made a point of regularly overflying the isolated Canadian Forward Operating Base (FOB) Martello, which was situated in a remote area to the north of Kandahar. This was the scene of a number of kinetic events in support of the small garrison. On 22 October, two Harriers responded to a GCAS scramble in support of an Afghan National Army (ANA) unit that had come under heavy fire near Musah Qal'eh.

In the confusion of the ambush, three Afghan soldiers had become separated from the group, but the No 2 Harrier pilot was able to locate them using the TIALD pod. Over the following minutes the two Harriers fired CRV7s and dropped a 540-lb bomb that held back the Taliban until an AH-64 Apache attack helicopter could intervene and take over. The three separated Afghan soldiers were successfully reunited with the rest of their unit. Six days later, Harriers dropped an Enhanced Paveway II on to a Taliban-held compound near Tarin Kowt, neutralising the insurgents that were holding it.

During late October night CAS tasking took the Harrier pilots to Panjwayi (15 miles west of Kandahar airfield), Kajaki and FOB Martello. On the evening of 26 October, two Harriers were called to intervene after three Taliban insurgents were spotted setting up a mortar position near Panjwayi. After a 540-lb bomb was dropped into the treeline just to the south of the position, the enemy were seen taking cover in a nearby

Harrier GR 9 ZG505 flies over Afghan mountains in a typical configuration for later Operation *Herrick* missions. Two 500-lb Paveway IVs are carried on the outermost pylons, with CRV7 operational pods on the next inboard pylons. The AIRCM pod and the Sniper Advanced Targeting Pod are visible under the fuselage. The Sniper pod was a substantial improvement over the TIALD pod that it replaced (*Crown Copyright/MoD*) compound. The insurgents were neutralised when a self-designated Paveway II was dropped into the compound from 16,000 ft.

Two days later, a daylight mission was called to support an ISAF patrol that was under a heavy and sustained attack by mortars and small arms fire near Geresk. After the leader dropped an Enhanced Paveway II LGB on to one Taliban position, the JFAC confirmed that firing had stopped from that location, but that it had intensified from a second position. The latter was also silenced by a salvo of 19 CRV7 rockets fired by the No 2 Harrier. Two days later, another salvo of 19 CRV7s neutralised a Taliban group that had ambushed an ISAF patrol, once again near Geresk.

There was a welcome distraction from the stress and danger of combat operations in November when glamour models Lucy Pinder and Michelle Marsh visited Kandahar. In honour of their visit, two Harriers were decorated with images of the girls. Respecting the local sensitivities, the pictures were painted as silhouettes, rather than the classic 'pin-up nose art' that had decorated RAF aircraft in Iraq in previous conflicts.

Although the operational tempo in Afghanistan reached a peak in late 2006, it nevertheless remained at the same high pitch throughout the next two years. In 2005, the Harrier detachment flew 687 tasked missions (a total of 1358 sorties), of which just three per cent involved expending weapons, whereas in 2006 and 2007 the annual total was around 1000 tasked missions flown, with weapons expended on 12–13 per cent of those missions. In that time, the annual flying task rose from just over 3000 hours to around 5500 hours. The number of precision-guided munitions – Enhanced Paveway IIs – that were released over Afghanistan also increased from 17 in 2005 to 119 in 2007.

The arrival of No 1 Sqn in January 2007 coincided with the deployment into the Afghan theatre of the more capable Harrier GR 9. This variant carried the AN/AAQ-33 Sniper Advanced Targeting Pod that offered a substantially improved capability over the TIALD pod. The GR 9 also boasted the Terma Advanced Infra-Red Counter Measures (AIRCM) pod, which gave added protection from man-portable SAMs. From January, the Harrier detachment at Kandahar comprised two GR 9As and six GR 7As. Meanwhile, kinetic events in response to TICs continued apace. Working in conjunction with B-1Bs in each case, the Harriers dropped Enhanced Paveway IIs near Gereshk on 10 January, near Qurya on 24 January, near Sangin on 26 January and near Musa Qal'eh on 30 January.

Between 30 January and 4 February 2007, 42 Commando Royal Marines carried out Operation *Volcano* to clear the village of Barikju near the Kajaki Dam. The settlement was a complex of 26 compounds that were being used as a strongpoint by Taliban forces. During the operation Wg Cdr K A Lewis, commanding No 1 Sqn, scrambled from GCAS after the Royal Marines became pinned down by heavy fire from a compound. After Lewis dropped an Enhanced Paveway II into one compound, his wingman fired CRV7 rockets into three more compounds that were also being used by enemy firing parties.

AH-64s arrived on the scene shortly thereafter, but they could not identify their target. However, Lewis was able to mark the aiming point using his TIALD pod, enabling the Apaches to attack using AGM-114

Hellfire laser-guided missiles. By now the Harriers were running short of fuel, but before they recovered to Kandahar, Lewis dropped another Enhanced Paveway II into a compound that was being used as the Taliban headquarters.

Operation *Volcano* was followed by Operation *Kryptonite* on 10–12 February to clear the Kajaki Dam from insurgents. Both of these operations were precursors to Operation *Achilles*, undertaken by ISAF and ANA troops from early March through to the end of May to clear the Taliban from Helmand Province.

During a surveillance and overwatch mission in support of the ground operation near Qurya on 4 March, both the Harrier pilots and their JTAC noticed suspicious personnel climbing on to the roof of a nearby building. The JTAC believed them to be Taliban insurgents preparing an ambush, and this was confirmed when he came under small-arms fire. At this point the Harriers carried out a SOF, releasing nine flares as they flew past the insurgent position. This manoeuvre had the desired effect, and the JTAC reported that enemy fire had ceased and ISAF forces had moved into cover.

The next day, the Harriers provided surveillance of an enemy compound and known enemy firing positions near Sangin. Two weeks later, on 21 March, a pair of Harriers responded to a call from ISAF troops who were pinned down by heavy enemy fire coming from a hillside. They dropped 540-lb bombs and an Enhanced Paveway II on the Taliban position and fired CRV7s on to the hillside, successfully silencing the enemy fire. On the same day, insurgents were also active near the Kajaki Dam, and a building that was being used by the Taliban was destroyed by an Enhanced Paveway II dropped by a Harrier. Then, on 29 March, Harriers were called in by a JTAC to fire CRV7s and drop an airburst 540-lb bomb on Taliban firing positions near the dam. After these weapons were employed, the JTAC confirmed that the enemy fire had ceased.

By the beginning of April, the focus of insurgent activity had moved to Sangin. Harriers responded to TICs in this area, dropping Enhanced Paveway IIs on 3 and 7 April, while on 10 April a SOF was sufficient to deter Taliban forces from ambushing an ISAF convoy after it had been halted by an Improvised Explosive Device. A pair of Harriers had an extended engagement when insurgents ambushed ISAF ground forces near Gereshk on 25 May. The Harriers were called in to fire CRV7s at the enemy position, which was in a tree line. The JTAC confirmed hits, and he also relayed the ground commander's request to attack another hostile group that was advancing in their direction. The enemy group was halted by CRV7s and an Enhanced Paveway II, but the Harrier pilots were then asked to destroy a building inside an enemy compound. This was achieved with another Enhanced Paveway II.

However, a further enemy position had opened fire on the ISAF force with mortars. The Harriers also neutralised the mortar position with CRV7s and then bombed an enemy compound with Enhanced Paveway II and fired rockets at another group of insurgents as they approached the ISAF troops. After this, the JTAC reported all enemy activity in the vicinity had finally ceased.

The 500-lb Paveway IV was introduced in Afghanistan in November 2007, and it quickly became the weapon of choice. The LGB's smaller size in relation to the Paveway II meant that it could be used in circumstances where the heavier weapon would cause too much collateral damage or risk injury to friendly forces on the ground. On the next pylon is a CRV7 operational pod – the rockets are protected by a frangible nose cap (*Crown Copyright/MoD*)

Taliban activity dropped off slightly during the summer when No 4 Sqn took over between June and October. Although CRV7 rockets were fired on occasions throughout the deployment, a SOF was usually sufficient to break a TIC or deter an ambush. However, the pace picked up again in the autumn. The Naval Strike Wing (formerly 800 NAS) took over from No 4 Sqn in October, and Harriers used CRV7s to break a TIC near Deh Rawood (seven miles north of Kandahar) on 19 November.

Four days later, a pair of Harriers worked with A-10s and F-15Es in the Deh Rawood area again, dropping an Enhanced Paveway II and a 540-lb bomb, as well as firing CRV7s at enemy positions. That same day also saw another Harrier pair called to neutralise a Taliban mortar position, a group of insurgents and an enemy structure near Asadabad, close to the border with Pakistan. The task was achieved by dropping both an Enhanced Paveway II and a 540-lb bomb, as well as firing CRV7s.

From November, the 500-lb Paveway IV LGB became available for the Harrier GR 9. This bomb added to the operational flexibility of the new aircraft variant, being a more suitable weapon than the larger Enhanced Paveway II when there was a need to minimise collateral damage. On 4 December, a Harrier GR 9A employed an Enhanced Paveway II, a 540-lb bomb and CRV7 rockets to stop a vehicle that was transporting enemy personnel to the southwest of Kandahar. A GR 9A also attacked an enemy position near Musa Qal'eh with an Enhanced Paveway II, before carrying out a SOF to deter further hostile activity.

Over the following ten days, SOFs were flown over Musa Qal'eh, Sangin, the Kajaki Dam and Kandahar. CRV7s and an Enhanced Paveway II were expended at Deh Rawood on 7 December, and ten days

later a pair of Harrier GR 7As coordinated with French Mirage 2000s at Orgun-e, dropping a 540-lb bomb. The rest of the month was taken up with more SOFs – over Kandahar (by a GR 7A on 17 December), Musa Qal'eh (by GR 9As on 20 and 22 December), Now Zad (by a GR 9A on 22 December), Deh Rawood (by a GR 7A on 27 December) and Sangin (by GR 9As on 29 December).

There were two kinetic events on 23 January 2008, with a Harrier used an Enhanced Paveway II to destroy an ISAF vehicle that had broken down near Sangin in order to deny its use to the enemy, while another Harrier used an Enhanced Paveway II, a 540-lb bomb and CRV7s to demolish a compound that was being used by insurgents. An enemy bunker system and weapons cache near Deh Rawood was also destroyed that day by a Harrier using an Enhanced Paveway II.

No 4 Sqn took over responsibility for the Harrier detachment in February 2008, and on 10 February an aircraft was tasked to fly a SOF over a Taliban position near Gereshk in order to provoke telephone chatter from the enemy. This was to provide signals that could then be picked up by ISAF communications intelligence operators in order to determine the enemy's intentions.

Weapons events and SOFs continued through February and March, reflecting the high level and wide spread of Taliban activity on the ground. In two separate engagements on 16 February near Deh Rawood, one Harrier destroyed an insurgent position on a riverbank and another aircraft used CRV7s to target a building that was being used by a Taliban 'high value individual'.

In the following week, tasking covered the width of the country from Sangin (55 miles northwest of Kandahar), where a Harrier destroyed an enemy compound with an Enhanced Paveway II on 20 February, to Orgun-e, near the Pakistani border some 200 miles east of Kandahar, where another aircraft employed an Enhanced Paveway II on an insurgent

Three Harrier GR 9 pilots are in their cockpits waiting to start engines on the flightline 'at a base in the Middle East' in December 2008. The lack of bomb symbols under the cockpits and the fact that the aircraft are each fitted with four external fuel tanks under their wings suggest that these Harriers are being ferried to Kandahar as replacement aircraft (*Crown Copyright/ MoD*)

Harrier GR 9A ZD461 returns to Kandahar air base from a sortie in which it had accompanied RAF Tornado GR 4s on their first mission over Afghanistan on 24 June 2009. This was one of the last operational missions flown by the RAF Harrier force after five years of participation in Operation *Herrick* (*Chris Stradling*)

position on 23 February. That same day, a Harrier flew a SOF at Bermel (on the border with Pakistan, 60 miles southwest of Khost), and another Harrier fired CRV7s against a band of insurgents near Kajaki.

Sometimes multiple formations responded to TICs, and on 1 March Harriers fired CRV7s and dropped Enhanced Paveway IIs on enemy positions near Sangin while coordinating with B-1Bs and Mirage 2000s. Ten days later, Mirages were also present over Sangin once more while a Harrier dropped a 540-lb bomb on a Taliban mortar position. Insurgents were active around Gereshk on 31 March and 1 April, and on both days, Harriers fired CRV7s at enemy positions. Ten days later, a Harrier delivered an Enhanced Paveway II on insurgents operating near Zaranj, on the western border with Iran.

April 2008 also saw the return of Wg Cdr Lewis with No 1 Sqn. At the end of the month and into May, Taliban insurgents focused on the area around Garmsir. Harriers continued to drop Enhanced Paveway IIs at approximately weekly intervals, but by now the General Atomics Aeronautical Systems MQ-9A Reaper Unmanned Air Vehicle was becoming the prime delivery system for LGBs. However, a Harrier GR 9A fired CRV7s at insurgents near Sangin on 15 May and then flew a SOF in the same area, and the next day a Harrier GR 7A dropped a

540-lb bomb near Farah, 200 miles west of Kandahar. This pattern continued through to August, when the squadron was relieved by the Naval Strike Wing. No 4 Sqn took over to cover the period from December 2008 until April 2009, when it handed over to No 1 Sqn for the final Harrier detachment at Kandahar.

During its final months in-theatre, the Harrier received a further upgrade in the shape of the Helmet Mounted Cueing System. Linked with HOTAS controls, this device used a reticule projected on to the visor of the pilot's helmet to enable him to slave the Sniper pod to any point of interest on the ground. The system made it much quicker and easier to identify targets on the ground, particularly when responding to a TIC incident.

From their arrival in Afghanistan in 2003, Harrier pilots had routinely flown steep departures and arrivals into Kandahar to minimise the threat from SAMs. As the Harrier force grew more experienced with operating from Kandahar, pilots began to fly the descending spiral 'anti-SAM' profile to land more and more steeply. On 14 May 2009, Flt Lt M E W Pert was leading a pair of Harriers on recovery to a busy circuit at Kandahar when he was told to expedite the landing because of the heavy traffic. Pert flew a very steep approach, but unfortunately even full power at the 'hover stop' could not arrest the rate of descent in the thin summer air. The aircraft landed very heavily, shedding its undercarriage and underwing stores before catching fire. The pilot managed to steer his Harrier clear of aircraft waiting to take off before successfully ejecting.

The early summer of 2009 in Afghanistan saw the launch of Operation *Panchai Palang*, a Coalition land offensive to drive out the Taliban from areas of Helmand Province. In the hours before dawn on 19 June, ten RAF Chinook HC 2 helicopters inserted 350 troops of 3rd Battalion Royal Scots into positions behind the Taliban defensive lines at Babaji, to the northwest of Lashkar Gar. The assault received overwatch support from both Reapers and Harrier GR 9As of No 4 Sqn.

Three days earlier, eight Tornado GR 4s from No 12 Sqn had arrived at Kandahar, and they took over from the Harrier detachment on 24 June. No 4 Sqn's subsequent return to Cottesmore from Afghanistan marked the end of 16 years of virtually continuous operational deployments by the Harrier GR 7/9 force, during which it had fought with distinction over Bosnia, Kosovo, Iraq and Afghanistan.

Despite these successes, however, and the many state-of-the-art modifications to the aircraft that had only recently been incorporated, the Harrier became a victim of the Strategic Defence and Security Review of October 2010, which brought swingeing cuts to British defence forces. The document stated that 'in the short term, there are few circumstances we can envisage where the ability to deploy air power from the sea will be essential. That is why we have, reluctantly, taken the decision to retire the Harrier aircraft, which has served our country so well'. So, to the surprise and deep disappointment of many, the Review had announced the complete disbandment of the RAF and Royal Navy Harrier force. The Harrier was formally withdrawn from service and the JFH disbanded on 28 January 2011.

APPENDICES
COLOUR PLATES

1
Harrier GR 7 ZG509/CH of No 4 Sqn, Belize International Airport, Belize, September 1993

When the Harrier GR 7 entered service, the aircraft was painted in overall olive drab that was identical to the colour scheme worn by the GR 5. Squadron markings were applied to the tip of the fin and on the forward nozzle duct. No 4 Sqn markings – a black and red rectangle split by a yellow lightning flash – had originated in the unit's days as a Sabre F 4 squadron in the mid-1950s. The aircraft is depicted here configured with MATRA 68 mm SNEB rocket pods on the inboard pylons and dummy gun pods. The 25 mm cannon intended for the Harrier GR 7 was never produced, and the obsolescent SNEB rockets were replaced by Canadian CRV7 rockets. The dummy gun pods were retained for aerodynamic reasons, however.

2
Harrier GR 7 ZG532 of No 4 Sqn, Belize International Airport, Belize, September 1993

ZG532 was one of two aircraft that had their tail fins painted in No 4 Sqn's colours as part of the unit's 80th anniversary celebrations in 1992. The rest of the aircraft is finished in olive green, appropriate for the low-level role over Europe. It is loaded with 1000-lb freefall high explosive bombs, which would be dropped on the range at New River Lagoon in Belize. During the short Central American detachment in September 1993, the Harriers used up some of the weapons that were kept in storage at Belize. For the short flights whilst in-theatre, the aircraft did not use external fuel tanks, so only bombs or Carrier Bomb Light Stores carrying three- or fourteen-kilogram practice bombs were carried on the underwing pylons.

3
Harrier GR7 ZG505/WJ (Operation *Warden*), Incirlik, Turkey, November 1993

With the move to medium-level missions for Operation *Warden* (also known as Operation *Northern Watch*), the Harrier GR 7s were sprayed with a temporary light grey ARTF wash over their original olive drab finish. No individual unit markings were displayed on the aircraft deployed to Incirlik air base in southern Turkey for the operation, as Harriers from across the fleet were cycled through for a few months during the entire detachment. Whilst at Incirlik, aircraft were allocated a tail letter preceded by a 'W' for 'Warden'. ZG505 had previously been assigned to No 3 Sqn, where it had worn the tail code 'AJ'. In later years it was converted to GR 9A standard. In this artwork, the aircraft is depicted in typical fit for an Operation *Warden* sortie over northern Iraq in the winter of 1993.

4
Harrier GR 7 ZG474/WL (Operation *Warden*), Incirlik, Turkey, April 1993

This aircraft is in the typical configuration for an Operation *Warden* sortie over northern Iraq in the winter of 1993–94. It is carrying a MATRA Phimat chaff dispensing pod on the outer underwing pylon, this store augmenting the internal Zeus ECM system to give the aircraft added protection from radar-guided SAMs and radar-aimed AAA. The CBU-87 CEM cluster bomb, like the Phimat pod, was originally procured for the Jaguar. In this artwork, the AAR probe is shown in the extended position, but for reconnaissance missions without tanker

support, the CBU-87s could be replaced with two more 2000-lb external fuel tanks. They would give the Harrier GR 7 sufficient range to cover the operating area from Incirlik.

5
Harrier GR 7 ZD406/WB (Operation *Warden*), Incirlik, Turkey, December 1993

After prolonged exposure to the elements, the temporary light grey ARTF finish became weathered and the original olive green scheme was visible in places beneath it. The typical underwing stores configuration for Operation *Warden* in late 1993 comprised a Phimat chaff dispenser pod (carried on the left wing outer pylon), two CBU-87 cluster bombs, two AIM-9L Sidewinder AAMs for self-defence and two 2000-lb external fuel tanks. In addition, a Harrier GR 3 reconnaissance pod or Vicon GP-1 wet film pod was carried on the centreline pylon between the dummy gun pods. This aircraft was originally built as a GR 5 and initially issued to No 3 Sqn.

6
Harrier GR 7 ZD435/47 (Operation *Vulcan*), Gioia del Colle, Italy, September 1995

By the time that No 4 Sqn deployed its aircraft to Gioia del Colle air base in the late summer of 1995, the camouflage scheme for the Harrier GR 7 had been standardised as a light grey finish overall. In addition, the practice of each squadron identifying its aircraft with an individual tail letter had been superseded by the allocation of a 'fleet number' for every aircraft in the Harrier force. Squadron markings were removed for operational detachments, but the groundcrew decorated their aircraft by painting white 'bomb' symbols beneath the cockpit on the right-hand side of the fuselage to record sorties where weapons were expended. In this artwork, symbols representing six LGB sorties and two 1000-lb freefall sorties can be seen.

7
Harrier GR 7 ZG508/79 (Operation *Vulcan*), Gioia del Colle, Italy, August 1995

This aircraft is shown in the configuration in which it was flown by Sqn Ldr Suddards when he led the first Operation *Vulcan* mission against the Hadzici ammunition storage facility on 30 August 1995. Suddards and his wingman, Flt Lt Holmes, were prevented from dropping their bombs by the poor weather on their first attack run, but were successful on a second attempt. The aircraft is armed with two 1000-lb Paveway II LGBs and two AIM-9Ls for self-defence. It also carries two 2000-lb external fuel tanks and dummy gun pods, although the under-fuselage centreline station is left empty. This weapons load was typical for many of the Operation *Vulcan* missions.

8
Harrier GR 7 ZG504/75 (Operation *Vulcan*), Gioia del Colle, Italy, September 1995

Clouds over the Balkans often precluded the use of LGBs, but sufficient accuracy against many targets could be obtained using freefall ordnance thanks to the Harrier GR 7's weapon aiming system. This aircraft is shown loaded with 1000-lb freefall bombs for a sortie against the EW site at Nevesinje on 7 September 1995. On this mission the aircraft was flown by Flt Lt Linney, callsign 'Sleepy 25', as the No 3 aircraft of a four-ship formation led by Flt Lt Cameron.

The Harriers delivered their weapons in a 30-degree dive against the target, which was defended by a S-60 57 mm AAA battery.

9
Harrier GR 7A ZD346/13A of No 1 Sqn, HMS *Illustrious*, June 2005

The Harrier GR 7A variant with an upgraded Pegasus Mk 107 engine entered service in 2003. The extra thrust available gave the aircraft much better performance when operating in 'hot and high' conditions, such as those found in Afghanistan. It also improved the handling and performance for carrier operations, an area where the GR 7's engine was stretched close to its limits. The GR 7A variants could be identified by the 'A' after the aircraft's individual 'fleet number' on the fin tip. ZD346 carries the markings of No 1 Sqn, which originated during the unit's days as a Hunter squadron. The unit flew its first Harrier GR 7 carrier sorties from *Invincible* in late 1997, after which it deployed to Kuwait for Operation *Bolton*.

10
Harrier GR 7 ZD401/30 of No 3 Sqn, HMS *Invincible*, October 2003

No 3 Sqn, operating from *Illustrious*, took over the responsibility for Operation *Bolton* in March 1998. The following year, the unit's Harriers also took part in Operation *Palliser* off the coast of Sierra Leone, flying once again from *Illustrious*. On 3 March 2005, two aircraft from the squadron, flown by Wg Cdr Offer and Flt Lt Townsend, launched from *Invincible* and deployed to Afghanistan. In this artwork, ZD401 is depicted in 'clean' configuration with no external stores, revealing the ventral strakes which eventually replaced the dummy gun pods. The unit markings, incorporating green and yellow bands, were first used when the squadron flew Canberra B(I) 8s during the late 1960s.

11
Harrier GR 7 ZD463/53 of No 4 Sqn, HMS *Illustrious*, August 2008

Like many of the Harrier airframes, ZD463 served with every unit equipped with the aircraft. Originally built as a GR 5A, it was converted to GR 7 standard and allocated to No 1 Sqn in the early 1990s. During the mid-1990s it was operated by No 20 Sqn, the Harrier OCU at Wittering. Later, it served with No 3 Sqn in the early 2000s and No 4 Sqn (as shown here) in 2006–08, before being passed to the Naval Strike Wing. The aircraft had also briefly been assigned to the Fast Jet Operational Evaluation Unit at RAF Coningsby, in Lincolnshire, in 2005.

12
Harrier GR 7A ZD327/08A of 800 NAS, Cottesmore, Rutland, January 2007

800 NAS was reformed within the JFH on 31 March 2006 after the withdrawal of the Sea Harrier FA 2 from service (with 801 NAS) earlier that month, although the following year the unit was renamed the Naval Strike Wing. The squadron colours are based on those carried by 800 NAS Buccaneers in the late 1960s. The markings on the forward nozzle duct were retained following the change of name to the Naval Strike Wing, whilst those on the tip of the tailfin were replaced by a black and white chequerboard – the marking formerly associated with 801 NAS. As depicted here, the aircraft has two bomb symbols painted in black just below the cockpit, recording recent operational sorties flown over Afghanistan in which an LGB and a 540-lb freefall bomb were dropped.

13
Harrier GR 7 ZD329 (Operation *Engadine*), Gioia del Colle, Italy, April 1999

Operation *Engadine* saw the Harrier GR 7s operating from Gioia del Colle once again. As had previously happened during Operation *Vulcan*, the aircraft wore a light grey colour scheme with no unit markings, and in this particular case without its individual 'fleet number' displayed on the tail fin either. By 1999 the Harrier GR 7 had acquired the capability to use the TIALD pod for laser designation of targets, rather than relying on the Jaguar to do so. Because of limited pod availability, however, Harriers operated in pairs, with only the leader carrying TIALD. The leader would carry out a self-designated attack and then illuminate the target for the No 2 aircraft. The TIALD pod was carried under the fuselage in lieu of one of the dummy gun pods, and it is just visible here behind the fuel tank. This aircraft is also loaded with two Paveway II 1000-lb LGBs.

14
Harrier GR 7 ZG530/84 (Operation *Engadine*), Gioia del Colle, Italy, April 1999

The introduction of SAAB BOL chaff dispensers, which were integrated into the AAM rails, meant that the Phimat chaff pod was no longer required, and so the outboard wing pylons were freed up to carry air-to-ground ordnance. This aircraft is shown in typical weapons fit for a CAS mission over Kosovo, loaded with four RBL755 cluster bombs. The RBL755, which was an improved version of the original Hunting BL755 weapon with a radar altimeter to permit delivery from medium-level, had its operational debut during Operation *Engadine*. Unfortunately, the weapon ballistics were not well modelled in the RBL755 aiming computer, resulting in ordnance often falling just short of the target. This aircraft is also armed with two AIM-9L Sidewinders for self-protection.

15
Harrier GR 7 ZD323/04 (Operation *Engadine*), Gioia del Colle, Italy, May 1999

Just as they had done in the previous conflict over Bosnia-Herzegovina, the Harrier groundcrew recorded weapon-dropping sorties by each aircraft with symbols painted under the cockpit on the right-hand side of the fuselage. Applied in black, this aircraft bears symbols representing five LGB sorties, ten RBL755 sorties and a further ten sorties on which 1000-lb freefall bombs were dropped. The aircraft is depicted with a typical load of four RBL755s and two AIM-9L Sidewinders, although the latter were not carried in the final stages of the conflict after it had been assessed that the remnants of the Serbian Air Force posed little threat to NATO fighter-bombers.

16
Harrier GR 7 ZD437/49 (Operation *Engadine*), Gioia del Colle, Italy, May 1999

The weather over the Balkans was not always suitable for LGBs, so many of the Operation *Engadine* missions were flown with freefall 1000-lb bombs. Like the RBL755, four 1000-lb bombs could be carried on the underwing pylons, as seen here. The navigation system of the Harrier GR 7 was updated using the GPS, which fed the precise positions of both target and aircraft into the weapon aiming computer, generating a very accurate aiming solution. Using this system, the Harrier GR 7 had the capability to drop bombs accurately on to their targets from medium-level through cloud. This aircraft carries markings indicating that it had completed six freefall bombing sorties, three RBL755 sorties and a single LGB sortie.

17
Harrier GR 7 ZD437/49 (Operation *Telic*), Ahmed al-Jaber, Kuwait, March 2003

Reflecting the lack of air-to-air threat over Iraq, AIM-9Ls were not routinely carried during Operation *Telic*, but the aircraft was fitted with four BOL missile rails (on the outboard pylons and the outrigger pylons) to increase the amount of chaff available to give protection against radar-guided SAMs. This aircraft is equipped with a TIALD pod and carries a 1000-lb Paveway II LGB under the left wing. It is also armed with a 540-lb freefall bomb under the right wing, which gave the pilot great flexibility in matching weapons both to targets and to the prevailing weather conditions, since poor visibility sometimes precluded the use of laser-guided weapons.

18
Harrier GR 7 ZD376/24 (Operation *Telic*), Ahmed al-Jaber, Kuwait, March 2003

After the conflict in Kosovo, the RAF published an Urgent Operational Requirement for an anti-armour weapon that would be more effective than the RBL755. As a result, the Raytheon AGM-65G2 Maverick missile was procured in February 2001. This version of the weapon had IR guidance and could be locked on to its target using the optical sensor in the Harrier GR 7's weapon aiming system. It was particularly useful when the visibility prevented the use of LGBs. As an alternative to carrying Paveway II LGBs and freefall bombs, the Harrier GR 7 could be armed with two Mavericks, as depicted here. RAF Harriers fired 38 AGM-65s during the conflict in Iraq.

19
Harrier GR 7 ZD408/37 (Operation *Telic*), Ahmed al-Jaber, Kuwait, April 2003

Although the AGM-65G2 Maverick had been procured as a replacement for the RBL755, the latter weapon remained in the RAF inventory and was used during Operation *Telic*. As the conflict progressed, the threat from Iraqi radar-guided SAMs and AAA reduced. This in turn meant that the BOL rails could be removed from the outer underwing pylons, freeing them up to carry bombs. In this artwork, the aircraft carries a TIALD pod under the fuselage and a typical mixed load of two 1000-lb Paveway II LGBs and two RBL755 cluster bombs (plus two 300-gallon external fuel tanks) on the underwing pylons. This aircraft is one of a small number of airframes that were decorated with a 'sharksmouth' during the conflict. ZD408 also has a bomb tally beneath the cockpit.

20
Harrier GR 7A ZD408/37A (Operation *Herrick*), Kandahar, Afghanistan, April 2005

There were few 'kinetic' events involving the release of weapons in the first months of the Harrier force detachment to Kandahar. During this period the aircraft were relatively lightly loaded, with a TIALD pod under the fuselage and the underwing pylons carrying four BOL rails, two 1000-lb Paveway II LGBs and two external fuel tanks. For a time, the Harrier Force adopted the procedure of loading all LGBs on to the inner underwing pylons, with the fuel tanks outboard of them because of lateral weight and balance issues with 2000-lb Paveway III ordnance. In this view the Paveway II under the starboard wing is largely obscured by the fuel tank. Since Kandahar is situated at 3000 ft above mean sea level, and it experiences temperatures of around 40°C in summer months, the extra power of the Harrier GR 7A became a necessity.

21
Harrier GR 7A ZD404/33A (Operation *Herrick*), Kandahar, Afghanistan, November 2006

In November 2006 the glamour models Lucy Pinder and Michelle Marsh visited British forces in Afghanistan, including the Harrier detachment at Kandahar. In their honour, two aircraft were painted with 'pin-up' nose art depicting the girls – although they were painted as silhouettes rather than colour images in order not to upset local sensitivities. This aircraft was named *Lucy* and featured the message 'Good work guys! Love & kisses, Lucy XXX' that Lucy Pinder wrote near the mission markings denoting kinetic events. The increased activity of the Taliban insurgency during 2006 is reflected in the large number of symbols – 19 LGBs and three airburst 540-lb freefall bombs. The aircraft is loaded with two 1000-lb Paveway II LGBs and carries a DJRP on the centreline.

22
Harrier GR 7A ZD437/49A (Operation *Herrick*), Kandahar, Afghanistan, November 2006

This aircraft, christened *Michelle*, was decorated with a silhouette of Michelle Marsh and the message 'Thank you so much. Love & Hugs, Michelle XXX P.S. Enjoy the ride!!!'. Its mission tally also shows evidence of many kinetic events undertaken by the Harrier force at this time. The bomb symbols record eight 540-lb ground burst and ten airburst freefall bombs, while the circular symbols show 21 attacks using CRV7 rockets. Two styles of silhouette can be seen, denoting the different types of pods that were carried on the aircraft. A typical fit would be a training pod containing six rockets beneath one wing and an operational pod containing 19 rockets beneath the other. In addition, 540-lb freefall bombs (with a mix of ground and airburst fusing) were carried on the outboard underwing pylons. The aircraft is also depicted carrying the DJRP on the centreline.

23
Harrier GR 9A ZD461/51A (Operation *Herrick*), Kandahar, Afghanistan, May 2009

The Harrier GR 9A was first deployed to Afghanistan in January 2007. This variant was equipped with the AN/AAQ-33 Sniper Advanced Targeting Pod which offered a substantially improved capability over the TIALD pod. The Harrier GR 9A also boasted the Terma AIRCM pod (not visible here since it was mounted on the right under-fuselage station), which gave added protection from man-portable SAMs. Featuring an impressive mission tally, ZD461 is depicted here in artwork loaded with CRV7 rocket pods and 540-lb freefall bombs outboard of the underwing tanks, with a DJRP on the centreline pylon.

24
Harrier GR 9A ZD433/45A (Operation *Herrick*), Kandahar, Afghanistan, May 2009

In this artwork of Harrier GR 9A ZD433, the Sniper Advanced Targeting Pod is just visible on the left under-fuselage pylon. The aircraft is armed with CRV7 rocket pods, which are mostly obscured by 500-lb Paveway IV LGBs loaded on the outboard underwing pylons. The Paveway IV was introduced to Afghanistan in November 2007, enabling Harrier pilots to attack their targets without causing unnecessary collateral damage. The tally of mission symbols beneath the cockpit gives a good indication of the workload of the Harrier detachment during the Taliban insurgency. This particular aircraft is now preserved at the Fleet Air Arm Museum at Yeovilton, in Somerset.

INDEX

Page locators in **bold** refer to illustrations.
Colour plate locators are marked 'cp.', with page
locators for plate and commentary in brackets.